Hawley Smart

Bitter is the Rind

Hawley Smart

Bitter is the Rind

ISBN/EAN: 9783744670722

Printed in Europe, USA, Canada, Australia, Japan

Cover: Foto ©Thomas Meinert / pixelio.de

More available books at **www.hansebooks.com**

BY

HAWLEY SMART,

AUTHOR OF "BREEZIE LANGTON," "A RACE FOR A WIFE."

" On serre l'orange ; on en jette l'écorce."

" Aimons vite
Pensons vite
Tout invite
A vivre vite
Pensons vite
Au galop
Monde falot."

IN THREE VOLUMES.

VOL. I.

LONDON:
RICHARD BENTLEY, NEW BURLINGTON STREET.
1870.

BITTER IS THE RIND.

CHAPTER I.

THE DE DRIBYS OF ST. HELENS.

ON the borders of that broad belt of woodland, which separates the fens from the wolds of Lincolnshire stood "St. Helens," the country seat of the De Dribys. It was a queer, rambling old house, of what can only be described as the composite style of architecture. The Elizabethan, with its sharp gables and mullion windows, perhaps predominated; but the old house had been added to so often by the whilom regnant, De Driby, as to have quite lost its original characteristics. The remains of a moat were perfectly distinct—indeed, parts of it had been converted into fish-ponds. The low stone archway still showed the grooves of the ancient portcullis, though the old drawbridge had been made into a permanent way.

A fine undulating park stretched away up to the woods, which formed its boundary on two sides of the domain. On the third lay a broken woodland country, while the fourth looked over a cultivated flat, terminating in the large alluvial track of reclaimed fen, bright on this April morning, of which I am writing, with the fresh green corn crops of that stiff clay country.

The De Dribys had been settled many centuries in these parts. Originally, in times long, long gone by, they had been vassals to the mighty monastery of Cottenham. In the days when the monks of Cottenham owned all those fair woods and pleasant undulating lands, stretching right up to the very edge of the now reclaimed marsh and morass country, the De Dribys had been "riders and reivers" at the beck of the then Prior of Cottenham. The Priors of Cottenham, in those times, had been Church Barons of great state and power, and the De Dribys had ranked as the principal of their warlike followers. Indeed, the sacred banner of St. Botolph and the whole of the armed followers of the monastery had been more than once entrusted to their keeping and guidance, and their well-known cognizance of "the bare arm and bloody dagger" had been seen in the front of most of the sanguinary struggles between the houses of York and Lancaster.

"They're a fell race, yon De Dribys," was a maxim of the country side, and in their annals were certainly few stories of their having erred on the side of mercy. Fierce, rapacious, and turbulent, they seemed to have mixed with it a species of prescient cunning or instinct, that ever prompted them to quit the falling cause precisely at the critical moment, so that they emerged from the stormy days in which their lives were passed with a constant accumulation of this world's gear in lands or plunder. In the early part of the reign of Henry VIII., a certain Sir Simon De Driby, who then represented the family, had arrived at great power and opulence; he bearded and even defied his liege suzerain, the Prior of Cottenham. Perhaps, like the vultures, he scented the coming slaughter. It may be the family instinct told him that the days of monasteries were numbered. Certain it is that he was an early professor of the Reformed Faith, and that when the dissolution of the monasteries took place, he showed that the reiving talents of his family had not in the least deteriorated. He swooped down upon Cottenham with his "merry men," as the cut-throat retainers of the brigand barons of those days were termed, turned the Prior and monks out of doors, and seized upon all those rich lands and pleasant woods for himself.

But there were a good many vultures aflight at that time, keen in the eye and subtle in the nose, for the picking of the monachal bones. Such a rich prize as Cottenham was scarce likely to escape their rapacious vision, and ere Sir Simon had finished the plundering of the monastery, he found two or three birds of prey as strong in the wing and as long in the spur as himself, who showing but little awe for "the bare arm and bloody dagger," were evidently determined to have their share of the broad acres and bonny woodlands.

They came, too, armed with strong injunctions of restraint from the Crown. Sir Simon thoroughly deserved the epithet attached by the country people to his race. He was "fell" as his most relentless ancestors, and the expulsion of the Cottenham monks had taken place under circumstances of exceptional brutality.

Væ victis—there is little mercy shown to the fallen, and those who for centuries had been the tyrants of the people, experienced but little commiseration at their downfall. Still, for men anxious to share in the plunder, it made a very pretty pretext—the unnecessary harshness that Sir Simon had used at Cottenham.

The subtlety of his race, however, still stood Sir Simon in good stead. He was not strong enough to resist, but quickly found the commissioners on his proceedings only wished to participate in the spoliation. He had, it is true, to disgorge in part; but, from his superior knowledge of the country, contrived to keep the lion's share in his own hands.

During the troubles of the Stuarts, the De Driby of the day long held aloof, finally declaring for the Parliament, yet he never had taken a part so prominent as to endanger him at the Restoration, so that the family tided through that stormy period without loss of life or lands, if without gain. It certainly was from no reluctance to plunge into bloodshed and deeds of violence, for there never yet had been a De Driby who had refrained from such, with little reck of life or consequence, should he deem his interests required it. The race, as a rule, seemed ever to have one end in view—personal aggrandizement. For this they had risked their lives and lands freely, and had proved stern, hard creditors when came their day of reckoning. I should rather opine that at the time of the civil war, the then De Driby had never been exactly able to see his way, that is, on which side it would be safest to embark, until a little too late. He erred, perhaps, from over-caution. It was an hereditary instinct of the family.

It is astonishing how people make their way who set up and religiously worship the idol of self-interest. It may narrow the general intelligence, but it makes it surprisingly acute on that one particular point. That was the great creed of the De Dribys.

> "And whatsoever king shall reign,
> I'll still be Vicar of Bray, Sirs."

Firm adherence to this belief saw them through the Jacobite troubles, though a De Driby in those days slightly compromised himself from a premature belief that,

> "The King would enjoy his own again;"

but he backed out in time, and still the family flourished.

Their knell was, however, ringing. Never had they owned more broad acres, or been in receipt of a larger annual income than when George III was king; but Sir Ralph, the present baronet's father, had the old blood in him still. It is true, the days of reiving, spoliation and assignment were gone—there were no monasteries to plunder—no lands to be given for service rendered—no attainted estates in the market for those who faithfully adhered to the House of Hanover; but the dice-box was ringing at White's, and Fox and my Lord Rivers were losing their thousands at a sitting. Sir Ralph played with the boldest of that gambling crew. He played with all the persistent energy of his race—impassable in his moments of victory as in those of defeat. His dark saturnine aspect at first produced some raillery amongst that witty and reckless circle; but the readiness and accuracy of Sir Ralph's pistol soon proved the danger of jesting with a man who had no appreciation of humour, and was full as "fell" as the worst of his family. Still the old marauding spirit was strong in him, and it was not till many a goodly acre was shorn from the family property, that Sir Ralph came to the conclusion that the dice-box was a robber on a bigger scale than himself, and with whose power it was hopeless to cope. The natural instinct of the family still showed itself, for he contrived to marry an heiress whose fortune went a considerable way towards the rescue of his entangled estate.

Sir Ralph having taken unto himself a wife, then betook himself to St. Helens, and compensated himself for his reverses at White's, by harrying his tenants and waging a fierce internecine war with the poachers—pursuits which, in those days, entered largely into the lives of most country gentlemen.

Sir Ralph was blessed or afflicted (it is, you see, such a perfect matter of chance which way it turns out) with two sons and three daughters. The sons followed much in the steps of their father, and were noted amongst the wickedest and wittiest set in the early part of the present century. In those convivial times just after Waterloo, when men drank port wine to about treble the extent their degenerate descendants imbibe light claret, the two young De Dribys were beating the watch, patronizing the prize ring, scouring the town, gambling at Wattier's, and getting drunk at "the Finish," with the *élite* of the land. Just as their race was about run, Sir Ralph betook himself off, as Dickens' cobbler observed "some-veres," and Sir Giles, the elder brother, reigned in his stead. Horace, the younger, with true family instinct, took to himself a wife, the only daughter of an eminent corn-factor, who had contrived to amass a very pretty plum in those days of war prices and prohibitive tariffs. It saved him from the Fleet, and after making her life a burthen to her for some half dozen years, he did the only thing left him to do in compensation, he died; leaving her with one son, named after his father.

Of the daughters of the De Dribys of this generation, the eldest behaved so indecently as to marry a well-to-do yeoman of the country. Great was the scandal when it was known that Sara De Driby had run away with young Alister Thorndale one fine May morning. Old Sir Ralph cursed them with most becoming unction, he was not at all the sort of father to omit that ceremony. Alister Thorndale disposed almost at once of his farm, and they were supposed to have emigrated to America. But Sara's name was never mentioned, and the De Dribys of the present day had long lost sight of her who had brought such dire disgrace on " the bare arm and bloody dagger."

The second, Eleanor, remained unwed, and at the time my story commences, was a quiet old maiden lady, living somewhere in the suburbs of London, while Jessie, the youngest and prettiest, the flower of the flock, had done what the sweetest blossoms so constantly do, married Sefton Merrington, one of the brightest, handsomest, and most irredeemable scapegraces that ever went through a nice property in some half-dozen years. Still, poor thing, if she had had her troubles they had been much tempered to her. Reckless as her husband was, he had loved her dearly to the last—compensation to a woman who loves for much misery; and when consumption cut the knot of all his difficulties, which it too soon did, she quickly joined him in his quiet grave in the south of France, bequeathing her little boy to the guardianship of his uncle, Sir Giles.

So much for the family history—I fear it has proved but tedious in the narration; but it is necessary for the understanding of this story to relate it. It is rather the fashion in these days to scoff at hereditary vices, or hereditary virtues; but "what's in the blood will out in the flesh." Breeders of horses, of stock of all kinds look for the transmission of certain points and qualities. Why are we to suppose that the human race should not follow the same law. With the exception of intellect, I think it undoubtedly holds good. "*Vous savez cette loi de la nation; le génie ne se transmet pas,*" quoth the great Napoleon. Some families transmit the same good looks from generation to generation, others the same violent headstrong temper, some tenacity of purpose, others dire vacillation. The De Dribys had always been characterized for most unscrupulous views, with regard to their own aggrandizement. It was the old fierce marauding spirit of the middle ages carried to an extent, which if exposed, the nineteenth century brooketh not.

There were few pleasanter rooms to be found than Sir Giles's own particular sanctum at St. Helens. An octagon, with three windows looking over the chase, with its gnarled twisted old oaks, not monarchs of the forest like their Northamptonshire brethren, for the light soil of the Lincolnshire woodlands produceth no such sylvan giants, but quaint weird-looking trees that seemed as if they had seen strange things in their time, and might unfold strange stories could they speak; oaks that you could imagine tenanted by some nymph or dryad of the forgotten old days—those dear superstitious old days, in which ghosts and phantoms were a reality to the men who lived in them. In these times we are taught it is all optical delusion, indigestion, or heaven knows what. At all events your friends refer you to science or the Polytechnic, if you mention such things. The dapple-coated deer raised their heads with that half-frightened, half-curious look, which compels one always mentally to compare them with primitive women, the hares leaped lazily over the grass, the rabbits were in their usual state of mixed fuss, impudence, and apprehension, and the regal old cock pheasants sunned themselves, and strutted before their plainer helpmates, as if the peacock on the pleasaunce was not quite the bird he thought himself, in their estimation at all events.

Seated in an easy lounging chair in this same pleasant octagon, this fine afternoon, is Sir Giles De Driby, the present owner of all this fair estate. A gentleman of the old school, but a gentleman *pur sang* every inch of him. Slight, pale, tall, with an aquiline nose, and piercing dark eyes, he carries his sixty and odd years well. The thin, compressed lips augur a man whom it would be by no means safe to cross, or take a liberty with, there's a fire in the dark eye, and a but half suppressed sneer on the lip, which, to the physiognomist, tell the tale of a bitter and sarcastic temper. Sir Giles, indeed, had lived his life in the fastest set of his time, and had imbued therefrom a cynical philosophy, the morality of which was at the lowest ebb. He was a disciple of a school much in vogue in his day, who scoffed at faith in man, or virtue in woman, and though the old vices had brought their own retribution, and gout, sciatica, &c., lashed him at times pretty severely, he still clung to the polished scepticism of his younger days. "Curses like chickens come home to roost," saith the Eastern proverb. This is probably an error of translation, "curses" should have been rendered "vices."

At the writing-table near the window an elderly man is turning over a mass of papers. They look a good deal like tradesmen's accounts, as, indeed, they are. This is Birkett Moseley, more commonly known on the country side as Birk Moseley. He is Sir Giles's agent, and at present engaged in deep conference with his employer on the subject of these evil-looking documents.

"Go on, sir," said Sir Giles. "Fifteen hundred and something, I think, was your last observation."

"Fifteen, forty-seven, nine. Whatever can he ha' done with it—that's what beats me."

"I dare say it does. With a De Driby for a mother, and Sef Merrington for a father. I can't say I see much cause for astonishment."

"But he declares he has never played, and you know—you see, Sir Giles—you recollect."

"Don't be unpleasant in your reminiscences, Moseley. It's astonishing how money-grubbers like you always contrive to make remarks out of season. The Israelite always reminds you your bill's falling due exactly when you wish to hear least about it."

"But fifteen, forty-seven, nine, and I've not got to the end yet, and—and—" he said.

"He didn't play. Don't suppose he did, or it would have been more. If he did, sir, he did it in such miserable fashion as neither his father nor uncle could be held responsible for. Gad! sir, the boy has better blood in his veins. *We've* played a bold game from time immemorial, and poor Sef Merrington was no craven at anything he went for."

"True, Sir Giles; and if ye'd not crowed so loud, nor flown so high, there'd have been more acres, perhaps, at St. Helens, and less mortgage than there is now."

"My dear Moseley, I have already animadverted on the peculiar deficiency of tact in your organization," said Sir Giles, blandly, as he raised his eye-glass. "Perhaps you'd be kind enough to arrive at the total as rapidly as is consistent with your astonishment."

"But if he didn't play, Sir Giles, what could he ha' done with it?"

"Went security for a friend, perhaps," sneered the Baronet; "or, more probably, conceived a *grande passion* for some precious daughter of Eve. Thought, as boys of his age are wont to do, that beauty in quiet silks loved him for himself alone, and has just discovered that your demure, angelic faces are to the full as vicious and expensive in their habits as their flaunty sisters of worse taste and more gorgeous apparel. But enough of this. Whatever the boy has chosen to make a fool of himself about, he has frankly owned it, and it happens to be my whim just now to put him straight with the world. What does it all come to?"

There was a silence of some minutes, broken only by the scratching of Moseley's pen, and the muttered ejaculations he made over his work. At last he paused, and observed:

"It'll be a matter of two thousand and a trifle over to settle the job, Sir Giles, and where you're to find the money, I don't rightly know."

"Raise it on the Cottenham fen lands," replied the Baronet, despotically.

"It's all very well; but I don't see how ye'll get any one to advance more money on them. I'm thinking they're mortgaged now about up to their full value."

"Well, raise it somewhere else, then.

It's your business to see how the money can be obtained."

"Like the rest of 'em, like the the rest of 'em," muttered Moseley. "It was just the way your father, Sir Ralph talked; and your brother, Mr. Horace, in his day was, aye, just the same. Find the money, and de'il mind what it costs. Stay a moment, Sir Giles," pursued Moseley, as he saw the Baronet was about impatiently to interrupt him. "I'm thinking ye'd better, if ye'd not object, have this money from me. I've saved a bit sin I've been the family agent, and if you'd gie me a small mortgage on St. Helens, it would be a good investment for me till such time as it suited you to pay it off."

"No, sir, I don't like the idea of mortgaging St. Helens."

"Well, then, I must try what I can do elsewhere; but it'd be the simplest way. Ye'll pay half per cent more to any one else, and ye'd be doing me a good turn too, Sir Giles, for I dunno where to invest my little savings rightly. Of course, ye'd pay it off just when it suited ye;" and here Moseley stopped and looked keenly at the Baronet.

"Psha!" said Sir Giles. "I don't know why it should not be so. A mere sentimental fancy that the old acres never yet have been under mortgage; the outlying property has always sufficed so far for such purposes. Sentiment is a weakness that should expire with our majority. Have it as you will, Moseley, and hark ye, the mortgage may as well be for three thousand as two while we're about it. A few extra hundreds will come in handy."

"Certainly, Sir Giles, certainly; that can make no possible difference;" and his keen grey eyes twinkled as he tied up the papers.

"By the way, you've got your daughter home again, I hear. How does she adapt her French airs and French graces to that old house of yours?"

Moseley's voice changed a little, and it

was in a more constrained tone than he had as yet used that he replied,

"My daughter, if she has had a bit of Continental teaching, is quite content to make her father's home hers. I reckon there's no great harm if she can talk their lingo and drum a tune on the piano."

"Not at all," said Sir Giles, blandly; "all farmers' daughters, and most ladies' maids in these days of intellectual development, at least profess such accomplishments. You must bring her up to dine here some day, shortly, and let me have the pleasure of hearing her play."

"Thank ye, thank ye. She's a good girl, Sir Giles, though you're always so full of your gibes at my having given her a bit more learning than you think necessary. But I'll be off now. Ye expect Mr. Fortie to dinner, and he'll happen be down by the afternoon train. She's been in long enough 'most for him to get here by this."

Even as he spoke, there was the sound of wheels grating over the gravel under the window, succeeded by the clang of the bell, and the opening and shutting of doors, and in a couple of minutes the door was thrown open by the stately butler with:

"Mr. Merrington, Sir Giles."

Fortie Merrington entered the room, and shook hands with his uncle and Moseley with the greatest *bonhommie* imaginable. There was not a particle of the returned prodigal in his manner. Not a sign that the catalogue of sins just discussed was the balancing of his ledger. But it must be borne in mind that Fortescue Merrington had come of age some few weeks before—had some small property of his own, and that when he submitted these debts of his minority to his uncle (also guardian), he fully supposed the means for their liquidation were to come out of his own resources, and, therefore, felt little compunctions regarding them. Sharp and bitter remarks on his folly, he, doubtless, anticipated; but Fortie Merrington was one of the few people who came in contact with Sir Giles who was not in the least afraid of him.

It had never been in Sir Giles to care much for his fellow-creatures in any shape; but as far as it was in him to yield to such weakness he had done so, in favour of his youngest sister and her scapegrace husband, Sefton Merrington. Their child, the bright, cheery, handsome youngster who, from boyhood, never seemed to stand in awe of him, had also won imperceptibly on his nature; and the household were wont to say, "Master Fortie might break the decanter, while the glass would cost his cousin Mr. Horace dear."

"Well, Mr. Fortie, I was just off as ye came in. Not but what I'm glad to 've had the chance to shake hauds wie ye; but you and Sir Giles 'll be for a clack now, so I'll just wish ye good-bye."

"Good-bye, Moseley; but mind, you'll

see me down the river to taste the home-brewed, and try for a trout in the mill dam to-morrow, most likely. I must see my old play-fellow, Katie, too. She must have grown out of all recollection by this."

"You're always welcome, ye know, Mr. Fortie, and Katie 'll draw ye the ale herself, though she does play the piano;" and the old man, who had not at all got over Sir Giles's sneer, took his departure.

"And so, sir, you're following in your father's footsteps, and have contrived to make a tolerable hole in your pittance before you have well come into it."

"Never mind that now, uncle. I'm afraid I've made rather a fool of myself; but we'll talk that all over after dinner. I'm off to dress now."

"Gad!" muttered Sir Giles, as his nephew left the room; "they learn their lessons quick in these days. Always take a narcotic before a homily. I presume the young villain thinks he'll bear my lecture best with a bottle of wine in him."

CHAPTER II.

THE NAIAD OF THE STREAM.

THE Rectory of St Helens was about a mile and a half from the Manor House, a large red-brick parallelogram, pointed with stone. Anything much uglier it would have been difficult to have built. The wayfarer, who took it into his consideration, oscillated much as to the conclusion he ought to arrive at respecting it—whether it was a poor house, or a Methodist chapel of some pretension. But when he looked at the prim garden, with its clipt yew and beech hedges laid out in the same uncompromising rectangular fashion, he felt intuitively that it was the residence of a clergyman of equally rectangular views, and suppressed his irreverent whistle. The genus tramp would have voted it most unpromising in aspect, and would probably have expressed their impressions in some such wise as, "Don't look a give away lot, that ere."

Such was the residence of the Reverend Horace De Driby, the son of Sir Giles's only brother. But though one may at times draw some inference, with regard to a man's disposition from his domicile, yet, in the case of the Reverend Horace, this would have been perfectly unwarranted, as he had only come into the living (a family one) some two years ago, and the Rectory and garden were pretty much as he found them. He was about ten years older than his cousin Fortie Merrington. A dark saturnine-looking man, of whom nobody professed to know much; quiet and reserved in manner, and of an apparently phlegmatic temperament, yet his parishioners had already found out that Horace De Driby had a strong will of his own, and held to his point with inflexible tenacity when his interest was aroused. For the rest, he was a type of the old orthodox clergyman, he preached two sermons a week, gave his poorer parishioners port wine, and half-crowns if they came to him in trouble, issued an organized dole of flannel and coals at Christmas, and interfered or troubled himself very little further with his flock, beyond the necessitous births, marriages, and funerals gave occasion.

Across the pleasant meadow lands, following the course of a bubbling sparkling brooklet, on his way to the red-brick Rectory, strolled Fortie Merrington, the morning after his arrival. He had had his lecture from Sir Giles over night; but it had resulted in little more than the inculcation of certain worldly precepts by that gouty Mephistopholes.

"What a jolly morning it is," said Fortie, to himself, as he paused to regard the stream with the eye of a fisherman.

"Jove! there ought to be a good trout under the willows there, just below the eddy. What a fool I was not to bring a rod. Ha! I thought so," as a sudden splash and swirl of the waters told that a trout of pretensions had emerged from his retreat, and was on the feed. "Never mind, I'll have a shy down here to-morrow," and he lounged on, carelessly watching the swallows as they skimmed and dipped incessantly in the brook. He stopped a second on coming to a stile, to watch a kingfisher in his panoply of blue and green, who was transacting a little business on the water on his own account, and then placing his hand on the top rail he vaulted lightly over and stood transfixed.

What signified trout, swallows, or kingfisher!—he had lighted on the Naiad of the stream herself. With hat thrown aside, 'neath the shade of the hedge, and apparently engaged in sketching, sat an extremely pretty girl. She raised her head from her drawing, upon perceiving Fortie, looked quietly at him for a moment, and then bowed. Fortie raised his hat with a puzzled expression, and hesitated. A smile flickered about the young lady's mouth, as she rose and said,

"What! Mr. Merrington, don't you know me? Have you forgotten your old fishing assistant?"

"Why, you don't mean to say—yes, you must be Katie Moseley.

"Yes, I'm Katie Moseley; you can't say I've grown out of recollection, for I'm sure I am not so very much bigger than when you last saw me;" and she glanced down with a smile at her own *petite* figure.

"No, but you've altered a good deal, you know. I can hardly believe you are the same little girl who used to come out and carry my bait for me, when I was a boy at Eton."

"Well, I've what's termed grown up since then, though I haven't come to much. You've changed too, Mr. Merrington, a good deal since those days, and paid more attention to your growing than I have done. It's very sad, isn't it? I always wanted to be tall, and I haven't achieved it."

"Never mind, Katie, you'll do very well as you are; but you take one rather by surprise, I forgot all this time I have been away that you have been developing into a young lady. I heard your father say something about it too yesterday."

"What," she replied, laughing, "did you still picture me as the little unkempt girl whom you used to bribe with goodies, to perpetrate all sorts of unfeminine feats in those pleasant old fishing times. Oh, dear, what scrapes you led me into. You don't know the weeping my torn frocks and wet feet of those days used to result in."

"Ah! I am afraid I encouraged you in most unladylike pursuits in times lang syne. I've a faint recollection of corrupting you by means of burnt almonds chiefly, and that there was a compo of chocolate and sugar could tempt you to face any wrath of the home authorities."

"Yes, you took terrible advantage of my weaknesses in those matters. I can recollect even now a terrible struggle with a big eel you had hooked, and how you comforted me when I sat down and cried at the dreadful mess I had got into in taking him off the line, with Everton toffee," and Katie burst out into a low laugh, as memory conjured up the picture.

"Ah! it was very wrong of me, though we had a deal of fun together all the same. I don't think I recognized what vials of wrath would probably descend on your poor little head when you returned home all wet and draggled. But what are you going to do now? Sketch on?"

"No, I think not, I'll go home now. You can carry some of my things for me, if you will. I suppose you are on your way to the Rectory; and so often as I've carried your fishing basket, I think you owe me a turn, don't you?"

"Only too glad. You'd better put on the hat though, the sun strikes hot. But what have you been about all these years, since I last saw you?" inquired Fortie, as he gathered up some of his companion's sketching materials.

"I have been at school in Paris the last three. I only returned about a couple of months ago."

"And how did you like that, Katie?"

"Very much," she replied, as they paced on side by side. "It was very pleasant, you know, to have girls of my own age to associate and talk with; at home here I had no companions, there I made several friends."

"And became awfully clever," chimed in Fortie.

"I don't know about that," laughed the girl. "I learnt a good many things of one sort and another. They didn't allow me to grow up quite an ignoramus, you may suppose."

"Ah, well, if they did their duty by you, Katie, as well as I did previously, you ought to be, as I said before, awfully clever."

"Oh, you!" she retorted, laughing. "I am afraid I had to unlearn all your lessons to start with. I don't think they would have quite appreciated the intelligence I had acquired regarding the use of a landing net."

"Useful accomplishment all the same. Still you must have had a pleasant time there, Katie."

"I had; there's only one drawback to it all, but I'm afraid I shall feel that bitterly. I learnt one thing more than was good for me."

"What's that?" inquired her companion.

"A mistake," said the girl seriously, "I learnt to become a lady."

"Ah," replied Fortie, in a somewhat puzzled manner. "Well, Katie, there's no harm in that."

"No, not exactly; but it is calculated to make life very *triste* for me in time to come. It's not likely," continued the girl, sadly, "that I shall ever be acknowledged as one about here. No, Mr. Merrington, father meant it for the best; but when I think upon it sometimes, I almost wish it had been otherwise. I turn off here; thanks for carrying my drawing-board. Good-bye."

"Good-bye, Katie; I don't quite understand you."

"No; well you will when you think about it. I hope you'll come and see us the first time the fishing brings you down near the cottage," and with a bright smile and little nod, Katie tripped across the hand bridge which led to her own home, and left Fortie to pursue his way to the Rectory.

"What a pretty girl she's grown,"

thought Merrington. "Don't quite understand why she should feel unhappy because she's been properly brought up. Should think playing the piano, drawing, and all that sort of thing great pull for women myself; you see they can't hunt, shoot, and fish like us. Jove! it is lines on them that, when you come to think of it. Crochet, croquet, and balls can't make up for it, besides we can do balls too. No, it's lines on women and no mistake," and still lost in the immensity of conjecture, that the enumeration of women's limited pursuits had aroused in him, Fortie knocked at the Rectory door.

Well, we are about to change all this. The great question of woman's rights is now agitated with considerable vehemence, and by the time they have obtained all they lay claim to, there will, at all events, be no cause to complain of lack of employment on their behalf. It may be that the women of the day are only a little in advance of their age.

> "Thoughts that great hearts once broke for, we
> Breathe cheaply in the common air;"

Still, I am afraid that the pioneers of woman's social change of status must make up their minds to leave unfulfilled one part, at least, of woman's mission, and die unmarried.

Mr. De Driby was at home, and Fortie was duly ushered into the study. There was no great sympathy between the two cousins, albeit they had always been upon good terms; the difference of their ages was against it, and although Horace De Driby was a fair horseman and tolerable shot, it was more the old family instinct that had made him so in his youth, than any real love of field sports such as ran riot in the blood of his more mercurial kinsman.

"Well, Fortie," he said, as they shook hands, "I suppose you've come down to spend some time with us now?"

"I don't know about some time. I've come for a bit; but, you see, there's nothing to be done much here in the summer, and I'm not a reading fellow like you."

"Not yet; but you'll perhaps become so. I don't think I was much in that way at your age. Besides, Sir Giles won't readily part with you for some little time. He's very fond of you, and has had but little of your society lately."

"Yes, dear old uncle, I think he's glad to see me, though he spares me none of the old cutting remarks. Not in him to let any one off those."

"No," replied the Rector, meditatively. "He's quite as caustic to those he likes as to those he dislikes."

"Yes. By the way, Horace, I met little Katie Moseley on my way here. Who would have thought of her turning out such a pretty girl?"

"She has grown up pretty, I am told. I can hardly say I have seen; just caught a glimpse of her in church now and then. Old Moseley, I fancy, has fallen into the usual mistake of the age, and entirely over educated her for her station."

"Jove! she looks and speaks as if she'd become any station. But I suppose that is it, she will find no fitting associates about here."

"None, if all I hear about her is true. He's made a lady of her; but that don't make a gentleman of him, and the country is not more likely to recognise her in that capacity than it is him. Social error of the day, Fortie."

"Ah! I'm not up in these problems. But what do you do with yourself? Now you've got the living, you're a rich man, and can afford those little runs to town you used to be so fond of. I should keep a curate if I was you."

"I do keep a curate, which enables me to go away for a short time as often as I please. I established one just before Christmas, a Mr. Phillip Filander. He's not over clever, but he does what I tell him, which is something, and seems to have no very positive views, except on the subject of his own personal attractions. He is always bewailing the dearth of ladies' society in these parts."

"Poor fellow! he's to be pitied down here, if that's his line. What some man at Oxford described as a *slippery* curate. No moral insinuation, Horace; it only means one of those white milk-and-water parties for whom the girls are always working slippers, muffatees, &c., and whom some young woman marries by violence in the course of three years or so."

The Rector smiled as he replied:

"Well, Phillip Filander I leave to take care of himself on that point. What do you think of doing, Fortie? It's getting about time you decided on a profession of some sort, isn't it?"

"Just what Sir Giles said last night. It's all very well to say you ought to do something, but what the deuce are you to do? Now, I can tell you quite easily what I don't like in that way, but can't for the life of me see anything that I do? Take the navy. Well, from what I've seen of ships, the accommodation is inferior. Shark-fishing, from all I hear, is not so good as pike. Shooting Cape pigeons and sea-gulls won't do after grouse and partridges; and then, Horace, how about hunting?" and here Fortie stopped aghast at the hardships of the naval profession.

"But you needn't be a sailor," said his cousin.

"No, of course not. But I'm always turning the subject over in my mind. I went down to Aldershot one day last year to see a friend of mine. It was a wet Sunday, and I only went because London was unendurable. Jove! he was living in a couple of cupboards, and the one where his bed was, leaked. I dined at mess, but it was the dreariest entertainment I ever saw. Everybody was yawning by ten, and looked as if they would like to go to bed, but I suppose their cupboards all leaked too, so they sat up and smoked till it should stop raining. Don't think I should like the army."

"But a man at your time of life is lost without a profession."

"Good heavens, Horace! You're Sir Giles over again, without the claret. I suppose I shall be lost, then, whatever that means. I haven't head for the bar, and you've monopolized all the church preferment of the family."

"No use talking to you at present, that's evident."

"No, as Sir Giles said last night in his pleasant way, 'As you're endowed with a mind, I presume you were sent into this world for some wise purpose, which at present appears inscrutable.'"

"And what, may I ask, did you say to that?" inquired the Rector.

"Roared, Horace, as I replied, 'Quite right, uncle, but not at all inscrutable. 'Forty-eight claret was made to be drunk, partridges were made to be shot, and foxes to be hunted, and I was created for those three special purposes. Moreover, St. Helens seems a fit field for my labours.' "

"Sir Giles laughed, I presume?"

"Yes. He was good enough to say that I possessed impudence if I didn't wit, and that I should probably find it the better qualification of the two in these days."

"And that, I suppose, was about the sum of the conversation that passed between you?"

"Yes," laughed Fortie. "He remarked blandly, as he lit his bedroom candle, 'that, though I didn't seem adapted for anything else, he had never seen anybody so admirably fitted to tread in the footsteps of his progenitor and go to the devil as his father did before him.' With which pious benediction he left me to do a weed by myself."

"Like him, very; though he's fond of

you, Fortie, he don't treat you much better than other people."

"Perhaps not; but his bark's a deal worse than his bite. He paid an awful lot of money for me the other day, and wouldn't hear of it's being charged against my own little patrimony, which I fully expected."

"What! you've been in difficulties, then?" asked his cousin, curiously.

"Yes, I came to grief a bit," answered the other, curtly, "though that's neither here nor there. How is my aunt? and when is it you expect her down?"

"My mother wrote word she should be here by the afternoon train to-day?"

"Well, Sir Giles wants you both to dine at the Manor House the day after to-morrow? Will that be right?"

"Yes, half-past seven, I suppose," replied Horace.

"Exactly. He didn't say anything about the curate; but I should think he'd mean it. Will you tell him to come too?"

"He generally asks him when he has people to dinner, so I'll bring him."

"Well, good-bye, Horace. Give my love to my aunt, and for the present, adieu."

He lit a cigar when he got outside the Rectory gates, and mused a good deal over the events of the morning. Fortie, if he was not very clever, had a fair amount of common sense. He knew that Sir Giles and his cousin Horace were both right when they suggested it was getting time he made up his mind to do something. Out of the wreck of his father's property, there remained not very much over four hundred a year to Fortie, while he was quite aware that his capabilities of spending money very far exceeded that modest income. He knew that in the last three years of his life, he had exceeded the three hundred a year allowed him to the tune of a couple of thousand pounds, and he also knew that he had had the spending of pretty nearly his whole income. Sir Giles was very kind to him, it was true; but still Horace De Driby was his heir, and though scarce a third of the property was entailed, yet it was natural to suppose Sir Giles would leave most of it to go with the baronetcy.

As Fortie thought of these things, virtuous resolutions stirred him, he was one of those natures so strong in theory, so weak in purpose. It might indeed have been said of him,

> "In glorious morrows I am resolute;"

but the resolves of to-day melted like the hoarfrost beneath the succeeding sun. He was always seeing and determining what he ought to do—always postponing beginning to do it. It's a very every-day character, there's not apparently a germ of the heroic in it, yet these weak purposeless characters often, once or twice in their lives, stand out and show a power of that greatest of virtues, self-sacrifice, we would little give them credit for.

They do it too, generally, with a simplicity and single mindedness that strikes us all the more forcibly on account of their previously frivolous lives.

"Jove!" muttered Fortie (it was a pet adjuration of his) "they're right, I must be something. I don't quite know what yet, but I'll come to a conclusion before the month's out, there's no particular hurry; I can think it well over while I am down here, and in the meantime some of these trout want killing." He was walking along the banks of the stream now. "Oh! here's Katie's sketching nook. To think of the little thing who used to run about with me five years ago and help with the trimmers, growing up into such a pretty girl. She is pretty and no mistake. I'll go down and see old Moseley to-morrow, proper thing to do. Besides he asked me to come and try the old ale. Might be hurt if I didn't. Shouldn't like to hurt the old fellow's feelings. Known him all my life. What blue eyes they were." The last observation could hardly apply to Moseley; but Fortie, with all the casuistry of *vingt-et-un*, was cheating himself on the subject of a feminine attraction. As we grow older we admit it at once, but in our young days we ever try to humbug ourselves in the first instance, though we make up for it by the way we bore our associates on the subject shortly afterwards.

CHAPTER III.

A DINNER AT THE MANOR HOUSE.

MRS. DE DRIBY has arrived at the Rectory as expected, and has clasped her son to her breast in all the gushingness (if I may be allowed the expression) of her elevated nature. She is a woman on a large scale, and though on the wrong side of fifty not in the least inclined to admit it. She is wont to describe herself to her intimates as "all soul, my dear, and adoring intellect." The first part of which proposition is a strong argument in favour of materialist views, while with regard to the second one can only say there is much truth in the old aphorism, to wit that "people are apt to be covetous of that of which they themselves have little." The daughter of a nobody with reference to family, she had been married by a De Driby consequent on his necessities. She had had but a hard life of it during that short period, and nothing but the astute tying up of her marriage settlement had prevented her lamented husband from running through every shilling of her fortune. But if of humble origin herself, nobody could have more thoroughly identified herself with the family of her adoption. She could correct any De Driby of them all regarding the genealogical tree—the race were known to be proud of their ancient line, but no lineal descendant of "the bare arm and bloody dagger" had ever yet held his head so high, because the blue blood of many generations of robbers and reivers coursed through his veins as the widow.

It is breakfast at the Rectory. Mrs. De Driby having been properly got up by the sylph who presides over her toilette is languidly sipping her tea. Milkmaidish as she deems colour, she is forced to use a *soupçon* of rouge and a few other accessories to conceal the landmarks of time. Art must assist nature if we would fain look blooming in our eleventh lustre.

"And you tell me, Horace, that Fortie Merrington is down again at the Manor House?"

"Yes, mother; Sir Giles has been reckoning much on his coming. Has just paid his debts for him, so he told me yesterday. Don't look well does it?"

"No; but Giles is just the man to humour the whims of a scape-grace like that. He has a fellow feeling for wickedness and extravagance, it's a family weakness, my dear."

"Still, it would be hard if he carried it out so far as to leave nearly everything away from the title, and you know what a lot there is he can do as he likes with."

"Of course; but, my dear Horace, a

De Driby would be a De Driby, I should assume, to the last. Our race has never forgotten its obligations to its descendants. What our ancestors perished on the scaffold for, what they risked life and lands for, what in short—in fact, I'm afraid I'm too imaginative, Horace. You must bear with your mother's poetical tendency. I mean, in short, Giles could never think of doing such a thing."

"Impossible to say;" rejoined her son. "Nothing can be more unsatisfactory than my situation here. Few men, without speaking plainly, can indicate more clearly to another the position he holds them in, than Sir Giles. He has contrived to do that in a way no child could mistake as far as I am concerned. I am his nephew and the parson of the parish, nothing more; although, at all events, I must succeed to the Baronetcy and a modicum of the property, he thoroughly ignores me as his heir."

"It may be sheer ignorance on his part;

perhaps if I spoke to him he would see the thing in its proper light. As a De Driby, I am sure he would wish to see his heir recognized as such in the country."

"Better not, mother; Sir Giles knows his own mind and is ill to meddle with on any point, let alone this. No, mother dear, depend upon it, and I say this with all deference to your superior knowledge of the world, you will do no good by interfering. Simply count tricks into the enemy's hand."

Horace knew his mother well; without that little salve to her vanity it would have been hard to persuade her to hold her tongue, should occasion offer, as it was sure to do.

"Well, perhaps I had better not, at all events, at present; though I think I have some weight with your uncle. You recollect how pleased he was with that hint I gave him about the fernery last year. But, Horace, whom do you designate as the enemy?"

"Fortie Merrington, of course. He's likely though, I think, to cut his own throat."

"Good gracious!" screamed Mrs. De Driby.

"I speak metaphorically, mother. All I mean is that he is young and foolish, and that his father's blood runs riot in his veins."

"Sefton Merrington was terribly wild, but I hardly understand you, Horace."

"I only mean that I deem Fortie likely to succumb to the usual temptations of youth, and that his extravagance will ere long produce a breach between him and Sir Giles. If he does not, some slight assistance must be given him, that's all."

"What do you mean?"

"Mean! that I have no intention, if I can prevent it, of inheriting barren honours," replied her son, fiercely. "Mean that I have no ambition to be the first pauper baronet of my race.

From our respective positions in life, Fortie Merrington and myself stand as antagonists for an inheritance of near seven thousand a year. In justice it should be mine, and I'll not throw away any chance of that succession, because my uncle may be infatuated about a spendthrift boy. I shall feel justified in taking any steps that may further my ends in this respect. I feel that I am merely defending my birthright."

"But, my dear Horace, there can be no doubt about it. I don't think Fortie can be capable of any such designs as you would seem to insinuate."

"Pshaw, mother; you don't understand me. Fortie has neither brains enough, nor command enough of himself to work much detriment to me in this affair. But I feel instinctively that the ball is at his foot, had he sense enough to kick it. Look at the way my uncle paid his university debts the other day. Would he ever have done as much for me? He has cared always more about him than any other living creature. 'Tis what I said before, whatever we may be outwardly, from our social position Fortie Merrington and myself must be foes in reality."

These were not very christian views for a minister to hold with reference to his near relation. Still it might be urged in extenuation, that Horace had certainly never had any vocation for the Church. He had entered it, as, alas! too many men do, solely with a view to the easy income the family living would almost at once put him in possession of. The former rector was a very old man when Horace came of age, and Sir Giles had strongly advocated his preparing to fill the vacancy when it should occur. His mother had nothing left but the income her settlement secured to her. Horace was, consequently, entirely dependant on either Mrs. De Driby or Sir Giles, and the latter had pretty plainly intimated that nominating him for the living of St. Helens would be all the assistance he intended to render. Again, his mother from his boyhood had impressed upon him that he was the heir to the baronetcy and estates, and for some years Horace had viewed with jealous eyes the increasing partiality of Sir Giles for his cousin. He had brooded over it, as men of his reserved temperament are apt to do, till it seemed in his eyes a piece of flagrant injustice, that he was not already recognised as his uncle's heir. He felt that Jacob was already defrauding Esau of his birthright, and had finally worked himself up to such a pitch on the subject, as to feel almost justified in taking any steps that might preserve to him what he deemed his rightful inheritance intact. Consequently, when he learnt from Fortie that Sir Giles had paid his debts for him, the fact presented itself to his mind in the distorted light of an alienation of property that should justly, in course of time, have descended to himself—hence his bitter converse with his mother.

When he reflected on this conversation subsequently, he rather regretted that he had told his mother so much ; for though he had at present no devised plan for weakening Fortie's place in his uncle's regard, yet his common sense told him that his mother would be an eminently unsafe coadjutor in any scheme he might think fit to attempt. As he shrewdly conjectured, Fortie was likely to prove his own enemy shortly, with his sensuous, pleasure-loving nature and habits of extravagance. That uncles don't continue paying debts, and are wont to get irritable on repeated application, Horace was naturally aware, and from his knowledge of Fortie's character, he drew the conclusion that it would not be very long ere Sir Giles was troubled with a similar application. Then he thought, hazily, must be his time to widen the breach.

In the meanwhile there was nothing to be done, but to watch Fortie's proceedings both at St. Helens and elsewhere carefully.

It is the night of the dinner-party at the Manor House. Sir Giles is standing looking every inch *le grand seigneur* on his own rug. These dinners were wont to afford much mirth to the old man. His sister-in-law, if he did not get too much of her, an event which he took special care should seldom occur, was a source of intense quiet amusement to him. He delighted in drawing her out; her mingled affectation of dignity and intellect tickled the old cynic amazingly. He was accustomed to ask Moseley to dinner much as he would have asked his doctor, solicitor, or his smaller neighbours. Sir Giles, in his innermost heart, believed that he could count the people on his fingers who, in all Lincolnshire, were really his compeers. His conduct on these occasions was the distinguished condescension of royalty, and quite a thing to behold. Sir Giles, beneath his polished scepticism, concealed an unswerving faith in the greatness of the De Dribys generally, and himself individually. He never had done anything of note, but that did not prevent his believing there were very few things he could not have accomplished had it been worth his while. It was, perhaps, the intense stress his sister-in-law laid on the family dignity, coupled with the fact that she was not really one of them, that gave him such pleasure in her society.

The men who, like Sir Giles, sit with their hands in their pockets, and believe they can do anything they choose in this world, are innumerable. It is not till dire necessity compels them to face the collar that they realise the difference between doing and dreaming. They awake, then, to the sense of what labour means, and find out what drawing-room talent really is worth when brought into the public market.

Now, the presence of old Moseley had once or twice shocked Mrs. De Driby on these occasions. She bore with little patience that anything so plebeian should move

> "Betwixt the wind and her nobility."

The impracticable old man, too, was wont to make things worse by his utter abnegation of Mrs. De Driby's claim to be considered a superior being. When you reflect that Sir Giles, in addition to his annual joke of placing Mrs. Horace and old Moseley in juxtaposition, was about to introduce on the stage so *bourgeoise* a production as Miss Moseley; that, moreover, he had been previously informed she was very pretty, and quite the lady, you may conceive he was looking forward with great glee to the entertainment.

The solemn old butler announced Mr., Mrs., and the Misses Stephenson, and Sir Giles moved from the hearth-rug to welcome his guests. Mr. Stephenson was the rector of the adjoining parish—a genial, hearty man, blessed with a buxom wife and a couple of blooming daughters, fresh, fair, pleasant, honest country girls, much addicted to dancing and croquet. Then arrived Moseley and Kate, which, with the addition of Horace, his mother, and the Rev. Phillip Filander, made up the party.

Fortie contrived to take Kate into dinner without much difficulty, and the party were speedily immersed in the consumption of soup.

The announcement of dinner had followed so immediately upon Mrs. De Driby's arrival, and she had been, moreover, so taken up with greeting her brother-in-law and nephew, that she had had no opportunity of scanning the remainder of the party. But now she raised her eye-glass, and swept the table with her usual insolent stare.

"My dear Giles," she murmured, "I see you still think it incumbent on you to entertain that dreadful old Moseley. I should have thought his intense vulgarity would have sickened you by this. But who is that extremely pretty girl next Fortie?"

"Oh, she's only just arrived in these parts; promises to be quite an acquisition to the neighbourhood, doesn't she?"

"Of course, I can hardly say about that, as I haven't the pleasure of her acquaintance; but she is very good-looking, and dressed in very good taste. Who did you say she was?"

"I only observed, I think, an acquisition to the neighbourhood; but if you wish to know more particularly, Louisa, that is Moseley's daughter," and here Sir Giles glanced with an amused expression at his sister-in-law.

"Giles, you're joking, surely!" gasped the lady.

"Not at all, and I quite concur with you that she is a very pretty, well-dressed young woman."

"Young woman, yes, that's the term for her. What could have induced you to ask her here? My dear Giles, the housekeeper's room is the proper place for her, as the butler's pantry is for her horrible old father. The minx, too, to dare to dress herself up like that!" and Mrs. De Driby looked volumes of wrath at unconscious innocence.

Little aware of the black looks directed towards her, Kate was laughing and talking merrily with Fortie. I don't think I have described Kate Moseley yet. Look at her as she is to-night, for assuredly you will seldom see her to more advantage. A small but almost perfect figure, attired in white silk, with pale blue trimmings, which assorted well with her rich golden tresses, deep blue eyes, and clear complexion; hands and feet which protested against her plebeian extraction; but it was not in these rested the real charm of Kate Moseley—it was the *riant* mouth, the quick play of the mobile features, the rapid flash of the sparkling eye, all showing the quick, intelligent mind within, that constituted her real fascination; and, wanting these, beauty after all is reduced much to the lay figure one sees in some hair-dresser's window. She was but eighteen, yet few men, or, for the matter of that, women either, who, attracted by her beauty, had once been led to talk to Kate Moseley, ever left her side without a lingering regret. Clever and accomplished though she was, it was not that. It was more the quick, sympathetic way in which, almost by intuition, her mind seemed to resolve itself into yours. The stupidest of her father's labourers seemed gifted with an intelligence above himself as he talked with Miss Kate. Men always left her with the complacent idea that they had been more than usually brilliant during their converse with Miss Moseley. Still, as yet, but few men, and those certainly not of the higher educated order, had had much chance of being benefitted in this wise. Her marvellous adaptation of her own mind, one might almost say her own self, to the companions of the hour, was that rare gift we seldom see. It is not altogether associated with either talent or genius, and yet no foolish person ever possessed it. More a woman's gift than a man's, yet, as a rule, fatal to the possessor. Women of this class, with the choice of scores of lovers, invariably choose the wrong one.

I am afraid Hood was right when he wrote :

> " But alas ! alas ! for the Woman's fate,
> Who has from a mob to choose a mate.
> 'Tis a strange and painful mystery !
> But the more the eggs, the worse the hatch ;
> The more the fish, the worse the catch ;
> The more the sparks, the worse the match ;
> Is a fact in a Woman's history."

Men who possess it are generally voted the most pleasant people out ; but, in most instances, have gone irretrievably to the bad before they turn thirty.

Pretty Kate Moseley, at present, was oppressed with no such misgivings. It was very sweet to her, with her talent and education, to find herself at a well-appointed table and amongst gentle-folks. Her father's establishment was liberal enough, and Kate sole mistress thereof, for her mother had died some dozen years ago; but Kate had laboured in vain to introduce therein the refinement which comes by nature to those born to it. Moreover, it was a rich treat to be conversing with people who had been educated up to her own standard. I speak in a general way, for if truth must be confessed, I think it probable that Kate could have not only thoroughly extinguished Fortie, but have also reduced to dire discomfiture the Rev. Mr. Stephenson on many of the current topics of the day.

"No, libel! libel rank in the extreme, Mr. Merrington," laughed Kate; "though since we last met I have been to school, and learnt, I hope, a little. I can still relish all the dear old country pursuits as of old. I could still clap my hands and, I believe, scream with delight at seeing you kill a good fish, as I did years ago, when you landed that three pound trout in the mill-dam, and I held the net. Don't you remember how wet I got in the operation, and how you did scold because I missed him the first time?"

"Yes, I recollect it well. You were always wet, torn and dishevelled in those days, Katie. I suppose you are awfully proper now?"

"Well, if you mean I am not the untidy, harum-scarum little girl of those days, I trust not. I'm as fond of all that sort of fun as ever, but I've learnt to avoid tumbling into the water; that my hair looks better properly done up than flying wild about my shoulders, and that at eighteen the world expects us to be neat and nicely dressed, though it don't pay much attention to our proceedings at twelve."

"I suppose you learnt no end of a lot of things at that place you were at in Paris. More than I did at Oxford, I'll be bound. I learnt to row a bit, and rather improved my form to hounds and in tandem driving; but I think that is the sole result of my University career."

"Ah, well, I think I did a little better than that. I'd every chance, and one must have been very idle and very stupid not to have picked up something. Now, I don't think I transgressed grievously on either of those points."

"I have no doubt you have turned out awfully clever. When we get into the drawing-room, Katie, you must let me ascertain whether you are better on the piano than you used to be with a landing-net."

"Ah, Mr. Merrington, is time never to grant oblivion to my juvenile sins? Surely, as we captured that mighty trout at last, you might yield absolution now to those long past primary errors."

"Well; yes, right of arraignment, I think, may be fairly said to have lapsed. What was that? I beg your pardon, Mr. Stephenson, but what is that story that you have convulsed Filander with?"

"I was telling him a country-side story of thirty years ago. You know, Barnby Beck, Fortie? I'm talking of it before the bridge was built, of days in which the country was not so well drained as it is now, and when that ford, after a heavy downfall, was deepish to cross. In those times, our farmers and their wives often went about on the old pillion, lovingly together on one horse. A hale old man, whom I remember well, had been with his wife to visit some friends named Martin, at Hatley. They had dined with them early, passed a pleasant afternoon, and as the sun got low they started to return home. The good old lady was accustomed, as they say in these parts, 'to take her drops freely,' and after she had been duly hoisted on to the pillion behind her husband, the hospitable Mrs. Martin insisted on her having 'just a stirrup-cup;' the good lady yielded, and midst mutual good wishes they started. The soft summer air, the drowsy hum of the insects, and the sweet scented grasses and wild flowers proved irresistable, and long before they came to Barnby Beck the farmer and his wife were nodding. This mattered little, for the patient old horse pursued his way home leisurely. There had been one or two very heavy showers since they had last passed that way, and when they arrived at the ford it was much swollen. The old horse paused, his master only trumpeted in his sleep. Carefully did Dobbin essay the passage; but the water came up to his girths. The shock of the cold stream to their feet awoke husband and wife with a sudden start, their equilibrium was lost, and in a second the pair were soused into some three feet of clear running water. A tremendous splash, a struggle, and as the old lady regained her feet (still dreaming of the pleasant party she had left) she gasped out, '*No, Mrs. Martin, no, my dear, not a drop more on any account, thank you.*' "

"Capital, Mr. Stephenson, capital. Poor old lady, she was a splendid specimen of 'the spirit is willing, but the flesh is weak,' even in her dreams," continued Fortie, "her resolutions were virtuous."

"Yes;" laughed the narrator, "she's by no means the first backslider who has been brought to see the error of his ways by a douche bath of discomfort. A good homily might be deduced from that little story. Hope it will never come home to you, Fortie."

Mr. Stephenson had his own ideas on the subject of Fortie's character, and was not disposed to consider strength of mind one of his characteristics.

Here Mrs. De Driby, with a sweeping bow to the table, rose majestically and heralded the departure of the ladies.

"Pass the claret, Fortie, you young people, I know, affect abstinence on the subject of wines," cried Sir Giles. "The age soothes itself with the idea it don't drink, which simply means they have grown hypocritical on that point. In my younger days, I think we rather gloried in getting drunk—bad, stupid, I'll admit; but I fancy 'delirium tremens' claims its own quite as often now-a-days as it did then."

"Surely, Sir Giles, you must admit," said Mr. Stephenson, "that we don't indulge in the excesses our forefathers did in that respect."

"Don't admit it in the least—the vices of mankind really vary very little in all ages; but fashion regarding them does much. Drunkenness and intrigue were the fashion in my younger days. Light claret, intellect, and the march of civilization, are the mode now. Bah! it comes exactly to the same thing; those vices underlie the current of society now instead of running at the top, and with precisely the same strength as they ever have done. The decorum of one age is not the decorum of the next. This generation exceeds the last in hypocrisy, and that is about all you can say for them. Twenty years hence it will probably be the vogue to blazon your immorality again. An immutable circle, my dear sir. We glory one half of the century in what our descendants are ashamed of in the next; but the whole thing is a mere case of ebb tide or flood."

"Well, I'm glad to say, Sir Giles, that I differ from you *in toto*, and believe in our gradual improvement."

"Of course you do! we see it from different points of view. You, consequent on your profession, go on hoping; just as I, from my worldly point of view, go on doubting. But we'll drop the argument, Stephenson—have a glass of sherry and then we'll go to the drawing-room."

It was not to be supposed that Mrs. De Driby could afford even to acknowledge the existence of such inferior clay as Kate Moseley. She had seated herself with great dignity near the fire-place, and confined herself to patronizing quiet Mrs. Stephenson, who bore it meekly. But the good-natured Stephenson girls and Kate had collected around the piano at the other end of the room, and after a little talk amongst themselves, Miss Stephenson opened the instrument and played a lively set of valses—then Bessie, the youngest, sang an old English ballad, and finally Kate trilled out a little French *chanson* with such *espièglerie* and expression that Mrs. De Driby sat aghast with horror and indignation.

"My dear Mrs. Stephenson, I must apologize, but Giles is so thoughtless. Of course he never should have asked that Miss Moseley, any more than her vulgarian old father. But the idea of her having the impertinence to sing her abominable French songs here—I really must put a stop to it."

Supremely ignorant of that language, Mrs. De Driby had ingeniously demonstrated to herself that the acquirement thereof was totally unnecessary. Her argument was simple—she lumped French plays, novels, songs, &c., together, and pronounced them immoral. The people she regarded as imbued with a spirit of infidelity. Any thing French, therefore, unconnected with dress, was unclean and accursed in her eyes; and despite Mrs. Stephenson's deprecation, she would undoubtedly have interfered to prevent any repetition of such song on Kate's part, had not the entrance of the gentlemen diverted her attention.

"No; pray don't get up," exclaimed Fortie, as Kate rose abruptly from the piano. "I told you I hoped to hear you play. One song as a quittance of all your past misdeeds with the landing net."

"Better not," laughed Kate, "suppose I only aggravate those past and well-nigh condoned offences. Think what my situation would be then."

"Don't believe her, Mr. Merrington; she sings and plays charmingly," cried Miss Stephenson, with real honest enthusiasm. "Do make her give us another song?"

So Kate sat down again and sang the "Sands of Dee," with a weird mournful pathos that made her hearers' hearts stand still as she trickled out—

> "They rowed her in across the rolling foam,
> The cruel, crawling foam,
> The cruel, hungry foam,
> To her grave beside the sea."

"Yes;" said Mrs. De Driby to her brother, mid the applause that followed the termination of the ballad. "She is becoming more guarded since you have appeared; but really I thought I should have had to interfere before, did I not, Mrs. Stephenson?"

"Why, what did she do before we came in?" inquired Sir Giles, with an amused expression on his face.

"Oh! sang something dreadful in French, don't ask me—it was of Voltairean tendencies, I know it was. The flood of democracy that pervades the age is something too awful to contemplate. People seem to have no regard now-a-days for where Providence has placed them, and you, Giles, to encourage such a creature—you, a De Driby!"

"My dear Louisa, it strikes me if the democracy produce pretty daughters that sing as well as Kate Moseley, we shall all have to go—"

"Yes. I'm sure I don't know where," interrupted Mrs. De Driby. "I believe Bath is still considered aristocratic. In the meanwhile, perhaps you will ring for my carriage."

"In short, for the present," laughed Sir Giles, "you mean to go to bed."

"I am surprised that a man in your

position can jest on such subjects. The levelling tendency of the age is a thing to draw tears from—from—from the great Golgatha of Nations!" and, wrapped in all the satisfaction this tremendous peroration carried with it, Mrs. De Driby, her son, and her dignity departed.

"Miss Moseley," said Sir Giles, "you sing very nicely, have been well taught, and have by nature what can't be taught —expression."

Kate bowed, with a soft murmured "Very good of you to say so, Sir Giles. I am afraid there is more good-nature than honesty in your praise, as you really know what good music is, and I am afraid I hardly do."

"I say what I think, Miss Moseley," replied Sir Giles, curtly. "I always do; it's my way."

It certainly was, in one sense. His thoughts about his fellow-creatures were generally of a most cynical and acidulated order, and Sir Giles seldom deprived his associates of the luxury of sharing them with him.

"You sing like a siren, Kate," whispered Fortie, "and I'll never presume to think you stupid again."

"How good of you. I suppose I ought to curtsey. I have been taught to always on such occasions, as one of my governesses, a clever Parisian, used to say, 'Time spent in acquiring a good curtsey is far from being wasted. It is the best rejoinder a woman can make to a doubtful compliment.'"

"But I didn't mean that. I meant—"

"Stop; here's our carriage. You can tell me what you meant next time we meet. Good night. Good night, Sir Giles."

And so terminated the dinner at the Manor House.

"What a darling Kate Moseley is!" mused Fortie, over his cigar. "To think of that little dishevelled child turning out such a lovely girl."

"Pretty little thing, that Moseley," thought Sir Giles, in the privacy of his bedchamber. "Clever, too, and with style. How they acquire it, I don't know; but these middle classes come nearer to us than they did. It'll last my time, but I suppose the country will be a d——d republic or thereabouts by nineteen hundred. Fortie seems smitten. Wonder whether it'll be a bad attack? Bad for that Moseley chit, I presume, anyhow."

CHAPTER IV.

BY THE RIVER.

A BRIGHT May morning, and the sun flashes down on the winding streamlet, which sparkles back again its greeting to

"Day, the mighty giver,"

as George Eliot so prettily sings. The little river ran serpentining all through the Manor of St. Helens, and was fair to look upon that spring morning, although its willowy banks were flat, and rose but some three feet or so above its level.

"It don't promise a good fishing day, Mr. Fortie," observed the keeper, touching his hat, as Merrington strolled into the stable-yard in languid enjoyment of the morning cigar.

"No; too much sun and not enough wind, eh, Jackson? But I shall have a shy at the trout all the same. Which way had we better go?"

"Well, if you think good, sir, I expect we'll have as good sport down towards 'the deer leap' as anywhere; but it ain't likely trout 'll look at a fly much with such a cussed sun out as this, till towards the afternoon."

"All right; get the rods out, and I'll be ready for you in a quarter of an hour or so;" and throwing away his cigar, Fortie lounged back to the house, to see if his uncle was yet down, for Sir Giles was capricious in his breakfast hour, and, though seldom early, varied between ten and twelve, as a rule. He was late this morning, and Fortie had breakfasted without him.

He found his uncle over his tea and *Times* in the dining-room.

"Glad to see your aunt's lost none of her dignity. She's still as horrified as ever at the advance of democratic opinions—painfully afraid of returning to the class from which she sprung, eh, Fortie?" said Sir Giles, after the usual greeting had passed between them.

"Yes," laughed Merrington; "poor dear aunt Louisa firmly believes she was 'born in the purple.'"

"Natural! Commend me to a new peer for a thorough aristocrat. If you wish to convert a Radical, give him a place in the Government. They never stopped Wilkes' mouth till they enlisted him on the side of order, by letting him taste the sweets of a salary paid quarterly."

"The same principle as a reformed poacher makes a good keeper," responded Fortie.

"Yes, as Jonathan Wild and Vidocq made great thief-takers. A proselyte invariably becomes a persecutor of his former associates, more especially when a stipend is the reward of his apostacy. But where are you off to?"

"Going to try for a trout, though it's not a very promising day."

"Ah! you'll perhaps reach the Rectory. If you do, tell your aunt from me, my intellects get so confoundedly rusted down here, I can hardly follow her. Just ask her to explain what she meant by 'a Golgotha of Nations,' will you?" and Sir Giles chuckled grimly as his nephew left the room laughing.

Jackson was about right in his views of the day with regard to the fishing. Whether the trout were asleep, whether they were not hungry, or whether their flies were prepared "without a due acquaintance with the subjectivity of fishes," I can't say, but certain it is that the two whipped the stream perseveringly without a rise till they arrived at Gibbett's Nook, just opposite the Deer Leap. The spot was so called, because there, in the early days of the Georges, a noted reiver of the Marsh country had expiated a long catalogue of crime, and the peasantry at nightfall were still wont to hurry past the place where Piers Thornton "dree'd his doom."

"We may give it up for the present, Jackson. I shall go and smoke a pipe under that old clump of Scotch firs. I don't suppose the spirit of the old outlaw will interfere with us in such sunlight as this."

"No, we'll be safe enough now," laughed the keeper. "But for all that, I'd not care to be about them firs much after sundown."

"Why, you don't believe in ghosts? You don't really suppose you would see anything of Piers Thornton, if you were watching there at midnight, do you? I suppose you watch this ground as well as any other when the harvest moon shines bright enough for netting?"

"No, Mr. Fortie, we don't, and

wouldn't care to," replied the keeper. "There ain't no occasion either, for there's ne'er a poacher in these parts would draw net over these fields, or set snare in these firs."

"Why not?"

"'Cause its unchancy like. They do say queer things may be seen at dark in this very clump we're sitting in. I never saw any myself; but then, certain, I never went to look."

"Why, d——n it, man, you don't believe in such things, do you? You wouldn't be afraid, would you?"

"Well, Mr. Fortie, I'm afraid of no flesh and blood poacher that ever put foot in shoe-leather; but I gin into things you can't grapple with. Don't believe either this here Thornton at present, mind I'm not saying what he might have done times long since ever traps; leastways the birds, hares and things does wonderful well down this away. I don't like meddling with what I don't rightly understand. You, sir, at all events ought to be careful, for whenever he's seen he bodes trouble to your family, leastways to a De Driby; so my grandmother used to say, and she'd great knowledge, had my grandmother."

"Dare say she had; never mind, tell us the old legend, if you recollect it. If I ever heard it I've forgotten it."

"Don't know the story of Piers Thornton, your great grandfather, and 'the Spinning Nook,' Mr. Fortie you're laughing at me."

"Not at all, Jackson; I really don't. Go on."

"You know that little holt we call the Spinning Nook, which never was without a magpie's nest since I remember; times too as we've trapped, poisoned, and shot 'em off—you know that, sir, don't ye?"

Fortie nodded.

"Well, they do say them everlasting

magpies is the spirits of Piers Thornton, and the woman he murdered and died for." Jackson stopped to let this awful communication have its full weight, but his auditor smoked on tranquilly.

"You know nothing about the story then, sir? and what's more, them as knew the rights of it is all gone long since; but I'll tell ye as much as I knows. My gran'mother used to tell it this how: that years ago a good-looking woman in a red cloak arrived at St. Helens, and wanted to see your ancestor. She was a country woman like, but claimed to have a hold on the Baronet of some shape, leastways she wouldn't leave till she had seen him. She sat at the gate till he came home from his hunting, and when he saw her he said wrathfully, roughish-like, you know, 'What, you here, Maggie; how dare you after all I've said to you.'

"They say she answered him vicious: 'I've dared much for you, it's time you dared a little for me. I never heard of a De Driby who feared before.'

"He looked very black and angry at that, and bade her come in. What took place between them no one knows, but after half an hour she came out, turned on the threshold and said:

"'Let no one ever believe in your race from henceforth. 'Tis well I brought my spinning-wheel, for some one will need a shroud ere long.'

"She had left her wheel, it seems, in the village. On leaving the Manor House she went back and got it and some provisions. For the next two days she sat at the edge of that holt, and when passers-by questioned her, as to what she was doing, she only plied her wheel and answered, '*that which will soon be wanted.*'

"On the third morning that dark-eyed gipsy-looking wench was found at her post, with her throat cut from ear to ear, a broken spinning-wheel, and a half-made shroud lying beside her. How evidence brought the act home to Piers Thornton, how your ancestor pursued him with relentless animosity, how, in his endeavours to escape he took that desperate jump across the deer's leap, of which the foot-prints are kept clear to this day, you know, Mr. Fortie, as well as I can tell you. But they do say the murdered woman was either Piers Thornton's wife, mistress or sister, and that your great grandfather had brought her to shame."

"Jove!" said Merrington, "that's rather a good story, Jackson. I never heard it all before, though I have bits of it. But what do you mean about the ghost of Piers Thornton boding no good to our family?"

"Why, Mr. Fortie, you don't mean to say you never heard the old rhyme about Piers Thornton and the De Dribys?"

"Never."

"Why all the country-side as has got any learning and gumption knows that.

They say it's true too, though I'll not say I know that from my own knowledge.

"'When for nights three the sea aar* rolls,
Teeming with disembodied souls;
Shrieks Thornton round his leafless tree,
De Driby then his fate must dree.'"

"And you believe that to be the case?"

"Well, my grandmother did, and she was a knowledgeable person."

"Well, Jackson, I think we'll make another start again now, and work our way back to the Manor House. You'll have to give me timely notice of Piers Thornton being much about, so that we may lock up the plate, &c.; for from his habits in this world, I should think the spoons are the thing Sir Giles need be most anxious about."

"It's ill jesting 'bout such things, Mr. Fortie," said the old keeper, sulkily; he believed implicitly in the truth of his

* Aar—the sea-fog—a bit of the old Scandinavian tongue still in vogue in the fen country.

legend himself, and had told it with genuine earnestness. Consequently, he was not well pleased with Merrington's jesting observation.

The trout, as they fished their way homewards, seemed to have lost the Spartan fortitude and self-denial of the morning, and lost their lives in pursuit of a sophism, in a way quite worthy of mankind. It was with well-filled creels they arrived once more opposite the Manor House.

"Leave me the small basket, Jackson, and take the fish home. I shall work a little way further up stream I saw a good fish rise under the willows at the bend there the other day," and Fortie continued his way.

After two or three unsuccessful casts, however, it occurred to his mercurial imagination that he had had enough of it.

"Jove!" he muttered, "I'll go up and call on old Moseley, have a chat with Katie, and that'll about fetch one round for dinner. This old place isn't lively and that's a solid fact."

He put up his rod, and strode rapidly along now. It was probable that this thought was latent in his brain when he sent Jackson home with the fish. He soon came in sight of the dark red-brick gabled old house, all smothered with creepers and ivy, that constituted the agent's abode — with its garden, filled with bright spring flowers, running down to the clear fresh stream he had been fishing. Katie herself, occupied with some woman's work, was seated in the shadow of the porch, the dark shade of which seemed a fitting frame-work to the picture of her fair self, with her glistening tresses and light draperies. She did not perceive him until he had got within a few yards of her, when the crunch of his heel on the gravel, as he forsook the soft shaven turf, caused her to raise her head.

"Oh! Mr. Merrington, this is good of

you," smiled Katie, brightly, as she rose and extended her hand. "Coming to see me so soon, and also, I hope, to present me with part of the proceeds of the day's plunder. I like to think you haven't forgot the little assistant of 'auld lang syne.'"

"That would be ingratitude," returned Fortie, at the same time feeling rather embarrassed, as he reflected that the neat-looking basket slung across his shoulder contained nothing but the slight grassy bed on which the big trout under the willows should have placidly reposed, had he assisted that mighty fish to fulfil the destiny he had himself decreed. "But I am so sorry I have no share of the day's spoil to offer you, I sent what I had killed home by Jackson, as I passed the bend level with the Manor House, thinking I was sure to kill a good fish or two between that and here."

"And you haven't—oh dear! and the very sight of you suggested trout for dinner. Don't look so serious, I am not such a gourmand as to trouble myself much about it."

"Don't chaff, Katie."

"I suppose I ought to pretend not to understand that—but I do. Shall I translate it freely, now? French idiom, I presume for, 'put on your company manners, Katie.'"

"Why on earth can't you be serious?"

"What! because you have caught no fish. I don't see that is reason sufficient —moreover, I am in mood to be very much the reverse."

"No, I don't mean that; but let's talk sensible."

"*Merci, Monsieur,*" said Katie, as she bent her head low. "Did they teach the science of compliments at Oxford, and if so weren't you plucked, or spun, or whatever they call it? Oh dear; to think that my converse should be ever held anything else. I assure you I am not accustomed to be told so."

"Nonsense, Katie; you know what I mean."

"Perfectly;" laughed the girl. "Shall I tell you? You're puzzled, and can't quite make up your mind how you ought to talk to the little girl you knew years ago. Surely you might have found out the other night, that the little girl has grown up and takes her place as a young woman."

"Yes, and a very pretty one too. I told you so the other night. I recognized the fact there and then."

"You did, Mr. Merrington;" said Kate, more seriously than she had hitherto spoken. "Forgive me if I say you have not learnt the alphabet of life so thoroughly as I have. Last time we met you were three years my senior—now I am that older than you. Don't be angry," she continued, "it is ever so, a girl at eighteen is intuitively older than a man of one-and-twenty."

"I'll not object," laughed Fortie, "you

shall be any age you choose to put yourself at, Katie."

"You asked me to be serious a few seconds back, now listen to me. You treated me the other night with a certain amount of condescension. No woman, who is not a fool, ever bears that except from unworthy or interested motives. Your very compliment on my appearance savoured of patronizing approval."

That the young men of these days are not easily taken aback, I will admit. That the majority of young men of twenty-two would have deemed themselves perfectly equal to the occasion, I have no doubt. The lore and startling experiences that flow from their lips on such points in club smoking-rooms, and other places where men do congregate, are wont to humble quiet people like myself much. We suck hard at our cigars, and muse with flushed faces on our own surprising ignorance, concerning the ways and windings of women. But

Fortie, I am sorry to say, happened to be no more equal to the occasion than I should have been. It is so easy to assert what you would do or say under certain circumstances; but let the circumstances come like a thunder-storm upon your unprepared head, and you are mostly in the position of 'the man without an umbrella.' When the assault comes from a young and pretty woman, defence waxes difficult. Prettily knit brows and lustrous eyes, belonging neither to a man's wife nor sister, are wont to induce a feeling if not of guilt, at least of being somehow in the wrong, when the coral lips connected with them commence upbraiding.

"My dear Katie," stammered Fortie at last. "I'm distressed beyond measure. I'm sure I hadn't the slightest intention—"

"Stop, Mr. Merrington, and listen once more to me. Of any intention, I acquit you, else I had never talked to you n the way I have. But recollect, life is likely to be hard for me. For good or for evil, I've been brought up a lady—out of my station, if you will—still I intend to be either received as such or not at all."

Fortie was rather at a loss as to how to continue the conversation. He had been most decidedly caught without his umbrella, and began to think Kate by no means improved on further acquaintance. How was he to divine that he was expiating the sins of his aunt—that Kate was avenging the slights Mrs. De Driby had put upon her upon his luckless self. But so it was, and "the little minx," as Mrs. De Driby had termed her, was quite aware of the injustice of her charges, and that it was so. It is given to many of us in this world to bow our heads to the vials of wrath, that are reduced by a fellow-creature's short-comings. Woman has rather undefined ideas about justice, though her perceptions are remarkably clear as to the necessity of vengeance. As long as somebody is scalped on these minor occasions, she is not wont to be very particular as to its being the actual offender.

But now that her small vengeance was accomplished, and she saw Fortie much humbled and discomfited, Kate began to relent and felt that she must send him away, at all events, comforted.

"Now, don't look so penitent about it," she exclaimed, "and please don't be angry. I get a little sore about my position at times, and your aunt took good care to let me feel it last night. Come inside and let me get you a glass of the old ale as I used to do," and Katie led the way in doors.

Fortie followed; but this sudden change only still more confused his mental perceptions. From duchess to dairy-maid—from young lady of his own standing to old Moseley's daughter, Kate seemed to have passed in a few seconds. He thought he could talk to her now; "but, Jove! you know," he muttered, as Kate tripped out of the pretty parlour, "if I make a mistake she'll be on her stilts again in a moment."

She glided back in a few minutes with a tankard, and poured him out a foaming glass of amber-coloured ale.

"There;" she said, "I'm sure you must want that after such a hot afternoon's work. Tell me what you did and where you've been? I know the river well, remember."

So Fortie began recounting his day's sport, and was soon at his ease again.

"I am afraid you like neither my aunt nor my uncle, Kate," he observed, at length. "Beg pardon, I suppose I ought to say Miss Moseley."

"Now, you don't suppose anything of the kind, Mr. Merrington."

"Well, but if I call you Katie, I should imagine you ought also to call me by my Christian name, as in days of yore."

"Put with great casuistry," laughed the girl. "But, you see, it isn't quite the same thing. You may call a dependant like poor little me, nearly anything it seems good to your mightiness to condescend to. But, mind, though in consideration of our youthful scrapes, I'll allow Katie, yet the lower orders rise sometimes when too severely trodden on. So be careful; I've imbibed Republican ideas at Paris."

"That don't answer the question. Why shouldn't you call me Fortie?"

"Well, I should not so much mind, just between ourselves, and when I'm pleased with you; but in public, I dare not be so democratic. Besides, think of your aunt. It might kill her if she heard me address you as Fortie," and here Kate burst into a fit of laughter at the idea of Mrs. De Driby's face under such circumstances.

"Well, I know you don't like her," replied Fortie; "but that needn't hinder you and I from being friends."

"No, I should hope not, and though Mrs. De Driby did her best to spoil my evening for me the other night, she was unsuccessful."

"Oh! So you enjoyed yourself, then, Katie, after all?"

"Indeed, I did, very much. You were all very kind but her."

"Why, I thought I hadn't behaved, for one, as I ought to have done."

"Ah, never mind now. I've had it out with you, and was hardly fair to you, besides."

"Glad you admit that. Walk to the end of the garden with me, Katie, won't you?"

"Yes;" and the girl rose with her hat hanging by the strings negligently over her arm, and accompanied Fortie down the walk.

"And what do you think of my uncle?"

"He was very civil to me, and I've heard he's by no means that to every one. In his own house, of course, he's 'monarch of all he surveys;' but he'd be nicer if he didn't impress that fact quite so much upon his guests."

"How I wish he could hear your criticism! But I must say good-bye. Won't you say 'Good-bye, Fortie,' in memory of old times?"

"Mr. Merrington, your most obedient servant," laughed Katie, as she swept him a curtsey wonderful in its majesty for one of her small size. Then following it up by a laughing little nod, Kate Moseley tripped back to the house.

Regarding Fortie, one might say with Mercutio:

"O, flesh, flesh, how art thou fishified!"

CHAPTER V.

THE MANAGER'S ROOM.

THREE weeks slip away, during which, regardless of variations in the weather, Fortie continues to whip perseveringly for trout. It is seldom that he does not contrive but that his fishing shall lead him at some period of the day into close proximity with that red brick house by the river. It is a matter of course that he should look in. Katie, too, had always taken a great interest in the achievements of his rod. What more natural than that she should bring out a book and join him? At the expiration of that time, Fortie is hopelessly in love with Kate Moseley, although he has not as yet explicitly declared his passion. Kate requires very little information on that subject, but her feelings towards him are by no means so pronounced. She likes him better, certainly, than any one she has yet seen. It is only natural, as Fortie and the Rev. Phillip Filander are the only two young men educated up to her own standard with whom she has been as yet thrown in contact. She shrinks from the "well to do" young farmers who are occasional callers at her father's house, and these young gentlemen, by no means more diffident on the subject of their personal attractions than their betters, have quickly arrived at the conclusion that Miss Moseley gives herself airs. There is innate refinement about Katie, even had it never been cultivated. There are fine fibres in her nature that rebel instinctively against coarseness of manner, word or gesture. It did not jar the least upon her to talk to her father's labourers, but it did so very much when it came to conversing with her father's guests. More especially did the loud, boisterous manner and rather coarse jokes of the younger of them repel her; while she, certainly, on her part, rather alarmed them.

Shrewd and essentially sympathetic in her nature, Kate had rapidly penetrated Fortie's character. She knew already pretty nearly both the best and the worst of him. She had divined not only the gay, light, chivalrous nature that women are apt to so dearly love, but she recognised both his instability and weakness besides. Kate had made up her mind, not that she must of necessity marry, but that if ever she did marry it was essential for her happiness that her husband should be a gentleman.

On the whole, she was rather pleased when, having announced his intention of going to London for a month or so, he came to bid her good-bye. She rather wished to think matters over for the present, while there was little difficulty in withdrawing altogether from the position if she chose. So they two parted, with warm protestations on his side which Kate met, as was her wont, in that playful manner, half jest, half earnest, which, though it sometimes made Fortie very angry, yet after all had a strange charm of its own for him. So much so that, after the manner of lovers generally, he felt he would not, his irritation having had time to subside, have had her otherwise.

Possessed of a chair and a fragrant cabana, Merrington is lazily contemplating the kaleidoscope of "Vanity Fair," as it breaks into different segments or groups in the crowded Row, when a passing lounger, slipping his arm from his companions, crossed towards him and exclaimed :

"Fortie Merrington, thou infantile promoter of my juvenile comforts, once more welcome to Babylon. 'How came he thence —what doth he here?' in the words of the poet, or thereabouts. How are you?"

"Deuced glad to see you, Fripley.

Was thinking of beating up your quarters in a day or two. Suppose you are still in the old rooms?"

"Yes, for the present, the Temple still possesses its brightest ornament. Of course, I am still meditating that Belgravian palace that my wandering affections have recurred to any time these last five years. But the British public has not yet recognised my talents in a pecuniary point of view sufficiently to warrant that aristrocratic move. Besides, 'whisper it not in Gath,' Belgravia is pretty stupid in the season, and a desert out of it."

The speaker was a slight dark man about the middle height, clear shaved, with the exception of a well-trimmed moustache with quick bead-like eyes, that appeared to take in at a glance, not only all their surroundings, but even things that seemed without their ken.

Fortie had been Fripley Furnival's fag at Eton. There is not, you will say, much intimacy between an Eton fag and his master, especially when some five or six years divide them; but Fripley had always been kind to, and fond of 'the little un,' and Furnival was one of those public school heroes about whom their compeers predict such mighty destinies, and whom small boys regard as Alcibiades *resurgat.* Fripley had not, and as far as could be seen was little likely to realize these warm-hearted prophecies. He knew everybody in town, and he had done a bit of most things. All his friends agreed he could be anything he chose, but then you see he had arrived at the age of twenty-eight and still not chosen. He had written a few things for the stage, and had been successful. Many of the reviews recognised him as an acute and clever commentator. Magazines liked his articles, and society welcomed him cordially. Yet with all this, Fripley at eight-and-twenty was still no where, he wanted continuity of purpose—what he did, he did well, and in no way belied the promise of his youth, but steady resolute labour seemed quite beyond him, and it was useless apparently to expect sustained effort from Fripley Furnival. Men of this class, I need scarcely say are a very welcome addition to the genuine idlers of society, all more or less bored with themselves. A man who talked cleverly of most things, and might be at any time expected to do something really good and worth talking about was a man to know; consequently Fripley had no lack of acquaintances. He took all this just as it came, entered keenly into the enjoyments of this world, proclaimed himself a philosopher, whose theory was that all the roses you may gather are bare compensation for the thistles allotted to you, that he would make the most of his spring time, and when the autumn days came on, then should the world be edified by the results of his experience and observations.

Ah! it's no new theory that. Let me have my fling now, and I'll settle down to real honest work when it is over. It is little work we are good for when we have had that fling, and we are very chary of communicating our experiences to the friends of our *riant* days. A few weak men may whimper over their past days of sin and folly; but I think as a body we take our punishment in silence and humility, and have the grace to keep our feelings to ourselves.

"Sit down;" said Fortie, "and have a weed if you've nothing better in hand, we haven't met for months."

"All right, I'll tell you what we'll do, just smoke a baccy quietly and contemplate 'the raree show' here for half an hour, then you shall give me some lunch at the Areopagus, and afterwards we'll stroll up and see Brazeley Basinghall. I've a little business with him about three."

"Who the devil's he?" inquired Fortie

"Manager of the Hyacinth, not a bad sort—kind of fellow you ought to know as far as Brazeley has time ever to know anybody; but he lives in such a devil of a hurry, I can't conceive his even finding time to die. When he does, I should think he'd leave directions that he is to be taken by special train to the nearest cemetery, and that the burial service is to be as short as it can be made, as he is anxious about something or another in the next world."

"Rather a character," remarked Fortie.

"I don't know about that; theatrical men are always in a devil of a hurry to see somebody, without time to see somebody else. It's their normal state, though Basinghall's state of perpetual bustle is rather in excess of most of his class."

Many a bow and nod was bestowed on Furnival's chair, as the twain leisurely consumed their tobacco.

"Who's that?" inquired Fortie, as a good-looking, lady-like girl gave a laughing nod to Fripley, supplemented by a slighter one from her cavalier.

"That? Bessie Medlecott, of the Parthenon. She's first singing chambermaid there. Out of the bill to-night, I suppose, or else she'd be at rehearsal. That's Jim Driver, the burlesque writer, she's walking with. Rumour says he is sweet there, and he might do worse, for Bessie's clever, and a real good girl to boot. She'll bring grist to the mill in a couple of years or so. She's just got her opening, and works hard."

"Works hard!" ejaculated Fortie. "Why, you don't mean to tell me that actresses ever have to do that?"

"Weugh!" whistled Fripley. "Yes, 'young un,' though you, like many other people, seem blissfully unconscious of the fact, an actress, if she is ever to do anything in her profession, has to work as hard as a milliner, and with not a deal better salary at starting. Even after they've got through the drudging, they have plenty of hard work, though they're more fairly remunerated for it; but the work, my Fortie, sticks to them to the end, as it does in everything else that money is to be made by."

"By the way, I suppose you've got something else coming out, by your appointment with Basinghall."

"*Cela dépend.* I've been pretty fairly successful with two or three things, but managers are not fighting for my productions as yet. We call them 'groovy' people, because they so much prefer taking the work of an old hand to looking at that of a new. Of course they are right in a business point of view, and the public corrects their mistakes, as it does other people's on most points. No, my boy, there's nothing to test what your work is worth, as a general rule, like the value the public put on it. I don't say it was always so; but in these days a man is generally appraised at his fair value in his own time."

"Well, come along and get some lunch; the place is thinning," and the two strolled towards the regions of Pall Mall, in which the Areopagus was situated.

"And what line of country do you intend to take up?" inquired Furnival, as he leisurely sipped some highly-to-be-commended light claret. "A man in these days must be a millionnaire or something, you know. There never was a wider scope than there is now, though I'll admit there's plenty of entries for every stake."

"Scope!" ejaculated Fortie. "Why, unless you 'go for' the Church, the Bar, the Navy, the Army, or the Medical profession, what is a gentleman to be?"

"My dear Merrington," replied the other, in pitying tones, "now do be sensible, please, and drop all that exploded bosh about family dignity. The Howards, Montmorencies and De Dribys must awake to the conclusion that those glorious old days, in which such distinguished families were allowed license so unlimited that, as Hume expresses it, 'Thieving was not the peculiar habit of the low and indigent, but often common to them with persons of rank and landed estate,' are long gone by. The Montmorencies obtain their plunder legally now on the Stock Exchange; the Howards are conversant with the price of cotton. Come off your stilts, man, if you mean to talk sensibly."

"Well, look here, Fripley, without chaff. I should like to turn my hand to something. Suggest?"

"Hum!" mused the other. "There's comic singing justifies a brougham and pair of horses in these days. Now, don't get riled. I've heard you do 'The Ratcatcher's Daughter' very fairly in times lang syne. Then you might start 'the adventurer game,' political demagogue, or Exeter Hall; they all require nothing but implicit belief in yourself, and unlimited assurance. Men make very good livings out of all three, and become eminent people and of newspaper notoriety in following them. Don't be childish," he continued, as the other made a movement of impatience. "'Keep your temper, if you keep nothing else,' is a maxim that has pulled a good deal bigger men than you or I through scores of times since the world began. But come along now, and I'll give you my views about your future career on another occasion."

The two departed, and after a short walk up the Strand, turned up one of those smaller streets to the left, and arrived at the stage-door of the Hyacinth.

"Governor in, Collins?" inquired Furnival, as the janitor touched his hat. "Take my card up, and say I've come to see him by appointment," and like one of the initiated, Fripley immediately followed the dirty-faced boy to whom his pasteboard was at once transferred. They blundered down two or three all but dark passages, both up and down small lots of stairs, and the boy knocked at a door, with the observation to his companions of "You wait here."

"Come in, and be expletived," responded the energetic voice of the "despot of the realm." "Who the deuce is it? I can't see anybody. I haven't time. Fripley Furnival—tell him I'm out. Stop! His last farce went, didn't it? Then, of course, his next will be d——d. Expended the little humour he has in him in that last effort."

"It was a very good farce, and had a very fair run; you know it as well as I do," said a woman's voice.

"Don't know anything of the kind. How should I? I haven't time to recollect these things. Now, will you go? I tell you it can't be done."

"Yes; and I tell you it must be done and shall be done."

"Oh! very good. You intend to forfeit your engagement, I suppose, and say you'll not play it without those alterations?"

"No, Brazeley; I'm not quite a fool. I shall play it; but I'll play it down."

"Very good, miss, if that's your way of thinking. The sooner you seek another engagement the better."

"I shan't do anything of the kind. There's plenty of theatres in London, but I prefer this. The manager, I know, is about the most cross-grained old thing in town; but he did me a good turn at starting, and I haven't forgot it."

"Then why the devil can't you do what you're told?"

"Because I know better what's good both for him and for me."

"Well," exclaimed Mr. Basinghall, "I like you, I do—you, whom I brought out, and—"

"Who's been a credit to the theatre ever since. Now, listen to me for a moment. I can make nothing of the part without those alterations."

"But I tell you, the author will never submit to them."

"There, that'll do; you leave the author to me. Just ask him to attend the next rehearsal, and if he don't give in, I'll do all I can with it; I give you my honour."

"You're a nice article to have on the premises, upon my life you are, Miss Jerningham! After taking up a manager's time half of this morning,—you want to bully an author all to-morrow. There, do go, for goodness sake. I'll write to the author, and if he's such a confounded fool as to attend the next rehearsal, you may settle it with him. Now, boy, show Mr. Furnival in."

The two had been unwilling auditors of a considerable part of the foregoing conversation, and now, in obedience to their youthful conductor, entered the apartment.

"My dear Furnival, delighted to see you. Haven't seen you for an age. Never have time to see half the people I want to see," exclaimed the manager, a fresh, florid, dark-complexioned man of fifty or thereabouts. Miss Jerningham, I think you know."

Having shaken hands with Basinghall, and presented Fortie to him, Fripley shook hands with the actress. They were old acquaintances, and rather friends in their way.

"Glad to make your acquaintance, Mr. Merrington. Hope we shall be good friends when we know each other."

This was the manager's way; he always welcomed people cordially, whether he knew them or not. It was not altogether humbug on his part, for he was a genial, warm-hearted man, and had done many a kind action in the course of his career; but he saw in the way of business so many people, and made out of the way of business so many acquaintances, that he really hardly at times could recollect who he did know and who he did not. This general *bonhommie* was, consequently, a safe line to assume, and saved the hurting of sensitive people's feelings from deficiency of memory regarding their personality.

"It's a long while since I've seen you, Mr. Furnival. You never come down to see what we're doing here nowadays," remarked the actress.

"Well, I didn't come behind to congratulate you on your 'Rose Delmar' in 'The Ball on the Roll,' but I was there all the same on the first night to see it. Give you great credit, Lizzie; one of the best things you've done, to my mind, and, you know, I always have thought we hadn't seen the best of you. Rather hope we haven't yet, and don't think we have."

"Very nice of you to say so; but I'm glad you liked me in 'Rose.' It is a good part, and I tried hard to make the most of it. The papers all spoke well of me."

"I should think so. No more 'walking parts' now, Lizzie, eh?"

"No, indeed," said the actress, with a

saucy laugh. "Brazeley's beginning to see I've got something in me when I get a chance. Do you recollect how pleased I was when you persuaded him to give me that 'chambermaid bit' in your first farce. I have got a bit beyond that now," said the actress, with a saucy toss of her head.

"Of course, Your Highness. Still, Lizzie, though you're 'leading lady,' you'll have to do all you can with this thing of mine. It's not so good as 'Rose Delmar,' as a part; but you must do my heroine for me all the same."

"It'll be very bad if I decline to do all I can with anything of yours. When's it to come out?"

"I say, Basinghall, what do you mean to do about my comedy? When have you an opening for it?"

"Well, I really can't tell you. I don't mean to withdraw this 'Ball on the Roll' as long as it draws; and though houses are not quite so big as they were, it's still drawing very fairly. I've a comedietta of Sturge's in rehearsal, as Lizzie Jerningham there will tell you. When we've finished with that, we'll have a shy at you. I can't tell you any nearer. Managers must live, though actresses and authors seem to think they are only intended to introduce them to the public."

"Well, I shall look in again when I see that thing of Sturge's announced."

"All right, my boy; and now, 'pon my life, you must all clear out. I've heaps to do."

"Good-bye, Brazeley," said the actress. "Now, don't forget amongst your numberless avocations you've a lot of us to dine with you at Greenwich next Sunday week."

"Gad! I nearly had. I say, Furnival, you'd better come, too, and if your friend there will accompany you, I shall be charmed to see him. Now, please go, everybody."

A shake of the hand from the two

gentlemen, and a little nod from the lady, and the trio moved towards the door.

"Take my card in, you young cuss," said a voice with a strong American accent. "I reckon he'll see Seth Thorndale, and be glad to do it when he hears he's about his location. If he's engaged, ask for how long; he knows time's money as well as I do."

They paused as the before-mentioned boy opened the door, followed closely by a good-looking man about thirty years of age.

"Beg pardon, I'm sure," said the intruder, lifting his hat to Lizzie; "but I always stick to my card as close as a tender to an eng*ine* on these occasions. Only way, I tell you, if you want to do business. Hope I'm not interfering with you in any way."

"Not at all," replied the actress, with a bow; "we are just leaving," and she swept out of the room, followed by her companions.

"How air you, Brazeley?" said the new comer, as the Manager cordially shook hands with him. "Shocks to you, I opine, seeing me in this old country, ain't it now? but I've a piece all 'blue lights and sensation' running pretty slick the other side, and I did a biggish stroke in petroleum last week, so I reckoned I'd just run across and see if you'd anything here in the way of plays or talent that would suit, to fetch our Metropolis for the autumn. Our folks, you see, crave for novelty—express trains, blue fire, and a fellow on the line don't last 'em long. I like to pitch a drawing-room comedy into them after that, till they're on pins and needles for another dose of sensational excitement. Pity we can't get a chap to write us a real good slow poisoning piece. I think that would tell —not to prove fatal till the fifth act. Good-looking girl dying all through, you know, eh?"

"Don't care what brought you, I'm

devlish glad to see you ; but I've no time to talk with you now. No need to talk to you about a manager's business. Come and dine to-night. There's my address, Seth. Mind, sharp seven. Now hook it."

"All right, old man, seven it is, streaked lightning ain't a circumstance to the way I'll make tracks. Guess I've got an idea for you which ought to fetch the Britishers. Off she goes. Where's that young Nicodemus that showed me up, I'll never get out without a pilot."

Basinghall rang the bell, and the American manager, for such in truth he was, though he combined various avocations with it, departed.

"That's a devilish pretty girl," said Merrington, as after putting the actress into a cab, he and Fripley once more strolled westward.

"Yes, she is," returned the other sententiously, "and as good as she's pretty.

She lives at home with her parents, and, I should think, finds best part of the money. Her father is a professor of music, and teaches the piano, singing, &c., as far as he can, a good little man enough, but he don't make a big sum per annum at it. Whether he can't teach, or people won't be taught I don't know; but he's glad to take a turn in the orchestra here when they want an extra violin. Lizzie don't like it, and since her position in the theatre has improved, I fancy he don't often perform. As for her mother, she's now a confirmed invalid—ladylike woman, and I should think originally of better class than her husband; but I don't know at all who or what she was. Good-bye, you'd better come down to this dinner of Basinghall's on Sunday if you've no other engagement. Safe to be a pleasant party."

"Done with you, I'll call for you at your chambers about four."

"All right, once more good-bye," and

Fripley shot up one of those bye streets of the Strand leading to the river in pursuit of his own devices.

CHAPTER VI.

DOWN AT GREENWICH.

FORTIE is floating along on the pleasant current of London life. The question of what he is to take to for a livelihood is rather thrust into the back-ground just now, as a problem in no immediate want of solution. Plenty of time to think about that. In the meanwhile he is seeing something of life, and trying to discover for what avocation he may deem himself more especially fitted. It is not particularly calculated to harden the bone and sinew of character in its twenty-second year, this floating down the sunny sensuous stream of pleasure. It is very questionable too, whether Fripley Furnival is a judicious associate for a young man just launched upon town. Fripley meant to do nothing wrong when he introduced Fortie into the various sets of which he was a welcome member. They had done him no good, for whether literary, theatrical, or otherwise, Fripley mixed with the fastest and most dissipated of all. Clever people, too, they were mostly, whose talents threw a glamour over the real frivolity and uselessness of their lives. Many men who had done just enough, as he himself had, to show what they could be, if they would only give steady application, wanting which, genius however great seldom takes its place in the drama of life.

Fripley, and his associates too, had in great measure struck out their scheme in this world; they pursued it, though perhaps indifferently, and fitfully, still they did work to some extent. But Fortie glided along with them a mere pleasure-loving atom, seeking nothing, hoping nothing, doing nothing. The pursuit of pleasure is one of the most fatiguing of avocations, and the boredom inseparably from it a penalty bitter to render; but Fortie, still in the first flush of manhood, does not as yet feel this. It is to him as yet all a garden of roses, and "the canker i the bud" a discovery he has as yet to make.

It is with a light heart this bright June morning, that humming '*Ah che la mortè*' he jumps into a hansom and is whirled to the narrow archway of the Temple. He is going to call for Fripley, as agreed, to accompany him down to Basinghall's Greenwich dinner. Discharging his cab, he plunges into the intricacies of that legal community, and speedily gained the door of Fripley's chambers.

Responding to the "come in" which recognized his knock, he entered, and found Fripley and an associate languidly inhaling their tobacco after an extremely late breakfast.

"How are you, Fortie, my prince of revellers? Here's a day for Greenwich.

To the devil with your work-a-day world for the next twelve hours,

> "'Tis merry, 'tis merry in Fairyland,
> When fairy birds are singing,
> When the Court doth ride by the monarch's side,
> With bit and bridle ringing.'

Basinghall's our monarch to-day, and the fairy birds shall sing. By the way let me introduce you to Mr. Halden." Fripley's companion, a slight effeminate looking youth with chestnut hair, big hazel eyes, and an upper lip as yet devoid of down, half rose from his arm-chair and languidly acknowledged the introduction.

"Yes, it's a charming day for a run down the river," replied Fortie, as he returned Halden's salute.

"Sit down, have a smoke and make Halden's acquaintance, and in about an hour we'll start for the Temple of Whitebait and water-souché. True priests of Isis as any of the days of yore in which that voluptuous superstition flourished."

The Honourable Jim Halden, youngest son of my Lord Fieranford, was rather deceptive in appearance. Boyish as he looked, he had numbered some five-and-twenty summers, and there was but little of this world's wickedness in which he had not graduated. The youthful face with its hazel eyes and pleasant smile had already wrought "grief" to both women and men in its generation. Society rather eschewed Jim Halden, as a detrimental with the worst of characters. His male associates were wont to designate him as a loosish fish, which might be rendered that with an uncontrollable propensity to borrow, he conjoined an equally obdurate disposition on the point of payment. He had had a turn at pretty well everything he should not do; but had never applied himself in any way to anything that the world, looking at it in the most favourable light, (and it is wont too to make the best of an "Honourable,") could possibly recognize as creditable. He had bet with a magnificence neither warranted by the results or his limited income. He had displayed the same breadth of view, mixed with the same absence of mind, with regard to settlement in various play transactions. He was great in abnegation of principle, and sublime in indifference to the results thereof. It was a mystery to the many how he still carried on; but as Fripley once remarked, "as long as there's anybody in London with twenty pounds to lend on personal security, Jim Halden will never come to want." How it was that his numerous creditors allowed him his liberty, seemed inexplicable. But my Lord Fieranford had announced publicly, and in the emphatic language that that sporting peer generally employed, "that he'd be d——d if he'd stand to Jim any longer," so it may be presumed they thought extremities were useless and expensive.

The pale smooth face, and easy *train-*

ante manner gave not the slightest clue to his countless past iniquities. He looked, with the exception of a rather languid air, as if he had but a few months left Eton or Harrow. He chatted pleasantly with Fortie, the latter with his gay impulsive disposition was prone to convert the acquaintances of the hour into friends at short notice. He put down Halden as a man scarcely his own age, though in knowledge of the world the Honourable Jim was a good ten years his senior. Not a profitable acquaintance for a young man meditating on a profession, and yet it never occurred to Fripley there might be harm in bringing those two together. He knew Halden so thoroughly himself, it never flashed across him Fortie might prove less learned.

"Time we were off, at last," cried Furnival. "Run and get a cab, William. Better go by rail, I think, unless anyone's death on the river."

"River, I think," said Halden. "Comic

rather always on Sundays, you know. Couples 'on the spoon.' Materfamilias and her chickens 'on the out,' &c. Besides it's fresh air in a small way. I vote for the boat, what do you say Merrington?"

"Ah! I'm all for the water," replied Fortie.

"Be it so then," said Furnival, "come along, and we'll go

"'Down the ruby river.'"

The comedy suggested by Halden turned out a lamentable failure. It is hard to see the fun of a crush in which bad tobacco and babies are dominant, and the trio felt it rather a happy release when they made their escape at Greenwich pier. Of course Basinghall had not arrived. Men who live in a hurry are invariably behind time nine-tenths of their existence; but they easily made out their party, amongst whom they at once recognised Lizzie Jerningham, accompanied by an elderly actress, a Mrs. Crosse, by way of *chaperone*, and the Mr. Thorndale they had encountered on leaving the manager's sanctum.

"Fine day, gentlemen," observered the latter, "the old climate can do the thing handsome when it chooses. I rather expect one of the reasons you don't get such a flood of fine weather as we're accustomed to the other side, is that the weather's getting a little tired of being amiable so everlasting. You're all here any how; and the location's small, so you can't shift. But with us if the climate got cantankerous you see, why we'd up sticks and strike out for a new territory."

"Perhaps so;" said Fripley, a little nettled at the very free and easy manner of the interlocutor. "Here we use umbrellas instead of emigration when the weather is showery."

"Had me fairly," laughed the other, heartily. "I thought to get a rise out of you, and you've the best of it."

"How do do, Lizzie?" said Furnival, as he shook hands with her. "Oh, Mrs. Crosse, congratulations on your new line."

"What do you mean?" inquired that lady.

"Why, don't you know two years ago you devoted your great though mistaken energies to growing old. Charmed to see you have returned to your original avocation of growing young again."

"Fripley, my youthful adorer," rejoined the lady, laughing, "if you're not more guarded in your language, I'll carry you off and marry you, as sure as I'm a widow."

"Come here, Mr. Furnival," said Lizzie, "and tell me about this new comedy, and what I've to do in it. I am sure it's clever."

"You're right; there are two points upon which I've never had a doubt, one is my own ability, the other your thorough comprehension of it."

"Ah!" laughed the actress, "my comprehension has a good deal to say to it, you know, when we get your ability before the foot-lights. If I don't interpret genius nicely, I'm afraid genius might be goosed. But the British Public wouldn't treat me so now, I think."

"I should fancy not; between ourselves they've acknowledged your talents without quite making up their mind about mine. You needn't look down upon me though, I shall 'fetch em' yet. Recollect I sprouted first and helped you a little."

"Yes, I don't forget, and if the Lion isn't quite as big as the Mouse once thought him, the Mouse will do her little best to help him all the same. We'll make the comedy go, Fripley, never fear, when Brazeley lets us try."

"Ah! long live the king—here he comes, looking as if he'd walked all the way, and beaten the express two minutes. Got his wife with him, too."

"How do do—How do do, everybody.

Seth, my Trojan, delighted to see you. Fripley, you look as if you really did go to bed last night. Ah, Lizzie; a day that behaves with decency to bonnets, isn't it—the wife will be charmed to see you again. Mrs. Crosse, I'm ashamed of you if you keep on growing backwards in this fashion, you'll have to come back to the singing chambermaids of days gone by. How do do, Mr. Merrington. Glad to see you, Halden—come along up-stairs, I'm sure dinner is ready or thereabouts. Here waiter,

"'Go call for Bait, and let for Bait be called;
And let the caller thereof in his vocation call
Nothing else but Bait, Bait, Bait.'

Crononhotonthologos, my dears, or something like it."

Following the manager, the whole party trooped up stairs into one of those pleasant rooms at the "Ship," of which joyous memories remain to many of us. The party in all numbered some twelve or fourteen, and except Halden and Merrington were all more or less theatrical. Basinghall, with true dramatic instinct, called upon a stout gentleman, who was wont in the profession "to do the heavy fathers," to face him, and the party sat down.

Fortie found himself placed between Lizzie Jerningham and Seth Thorndale, and immediately devoted himself to the pretty actress.

"I've only lately had the pleasure of seeing you, Miss Jerningham, on the boards, compliments are superfluous, though I must tell you how charmed I was."

"Yes, you are quite right about compliments being a superfluity on that point; men always think they are bound to say that to us. No, the real compliments to an *artiste*, Mr. Merrington, are full houses, attentive audiences, a genuine round of applause here and there, and the laudatory criticisms of the papers. We believe the press when it tells us we do well, and our managers when they raise our salary. For the rest I put it down to the every day change of society."

"Yet you seemed pleased when Furnival told you the other day he liked your 'Rose Delmar.'"

"Ah! that is different; Fripley, you see, is an old friend and lent me a lift at starting. He is to a certain extent one of us, and in my early days was not the least reticent about home truths the other way. I own I was glad to hear he was pleased."

"Well, I must confess I know little about what you call the business part of the profession, I never saw a rehearsal. Never was in a theatre, before Fripley took me the other day, except to the stalls or dress circle. Till he undeceived me I had no idea that it was hard work."

"I daresay not, Mr. Merrington; very few of an audience have. Yet I have been on the stage at rehearsal from ten till three, gone home, been back at the theatre at half-past seven, not got away again till twelve, have sat up to study a new part then till near three, and been back once more at the theatre by ten the next morning, and shall probably often have to do so again."

"Well, sir, did you make a pretty fair 'collect' out of the Ascot business?" inquired Seth Thorndale. "As for me, the book-makers 'struck ile' as we say the other side; the dollars spurted out of my pockets into theirn in a most remarkable manner."

"Yes," said Fripley, "I went down and won a trifle, but I do very little in that way, you've been on the Turf in your own country I presume?"

"Yes, I've had a turn at that, not many things I haven't tried I think; you see when my father died, the mother, sisters and I, though we had enough to scrape along on, weren't left with a pile that's certain. There's an everlasting lot of ways of making dollars in most countries, but I reckon, as far as I've seen, that America tops creation for originality and versatility on that point. Our citizens, you see, change the groove pretty quick if it don't do. If we can't make one thing pay, we may another. I'm a theatrical manager just now of one of the leading New York houses; but it aint but a few years back I was 'running a chapel.'"

"What the deuce is that?" inquired Fripley.

"Well, you see, I leased the chapel, put in a good stirring parson at a fixed salary and then I let the pews. Yes, if you've a preacher that draws, it pays well that does. But our people are given to strong doctrine, and it's no use engaging one who don't give it them. Say, Brazeley," he continued, whispering across Furnival to the manager, "who's the old lady opposite, think I've seen her before."

"Mrs. Crosse. Very likely, she was engaged in your country for a couple of years or so, a good while ago. Used in her youth to do singing chambermaids, breeches parts, and a little in the dancing line, cachuca, hornpipe, provincial ballet and so on. Does the old ladies now, no great talent, but very safe. Real good utility actress in her way."

"Ah! a sort I wish there were more of. Difficult to find our side. They all think they're stars and the audience fools, when they don't draw. Suppose it's a good deal the same here though and everywhere else. 'Turn up your picture cards,' my boy, as Wendell Holmes says. we shall come at what you're worth then. The hand ain't much when you see it counted out mostly."

"No," said Furnival; "but geese will think themselves swans, and try to sing to the end of time. You and Brazeley there, I dare say, dispel a good many illusions per annum."

"Well, a man, or woman either, for the matter of that, ain't much unless he believes in himself; but there's two ways of looking at it. There's your soft, spongy, white-livered kind, who sit down and whimper when they don't succeed, and talk of unappreciative audiences. Digging, felling trees, and such like's the best cure for their complaint. But there's the other lot, who are real grit, who grind their teeth and say, 'You won't hear my play, or read my novel, or come to see me act; but by G—d you shall, and be thankful to do it, before I've done with you.'"

"Yes; no man need accept a first public verdict. They are generally fairly right, though, and if he succeeds, it is because he has done better the second time," replied Furnival.

"Beg pardon, Brazeley," said Halden, in his usual languid tone from the bottom of the table, "but if you'd let us have a glass of sherry, we might get to some coffee and smoke out on the balcony."

"Exactly. Quite forgot. Pass the sherry, Seth. Here, waiter, coffee, tea, liqueurs, cigars—everything. Have it in the balcony, eh? cool and comfortable; look at the ships, water, moon, and so on. Suppose there is a moon. Gad! if there isn't! I'd have had one down from the theatre, if I'd thought of it. You should see my moon, Seth; it's a stunner, I tell you, quite as good as the original in a limited district."

"Reckon I've a sun it ain't a patch upon," was that worthy's sententious rejoinder, as the party strolled out on to the balcony.

"No, Miss Jerningham, I haven't a profession."

"Not rich, and haven't a profession!" said the actress, opening her fine dark eyes to their fullest extent. "But what do you do? Don't you want money? We want so much now-a-days. I don't suppose you ever knew what it was to be poor, but I have, and, Mr. Merrington, I didn't like it. I'll never be very poor again, if work will save it."

"No, I've never known what it is to be poor."

"Ah, I see; your friends find you plenty of money."

"No, indeed, Miss Jerningham. I've only a small income of my own to depend upon."

"Then why don't you do something? It is so easy for men to make money—so hard for us poor women."

Fortie was staggered. The cynical expostulation of Sir Giles, the frigid remarks of his cousin, the laughing commentaries of Fripley on his want of a profession, had never moved him as did the quiet observations of the pretty girl at his side. Lizzie Jerningham looked very handsome in the fair sheen moonlight. No bonnet controlled the masses of her blue black hair, and the well-fitting silk robe showed off her lithe supple figure to great advantage.

"What a delicious evening it is," murmured the actress, as they stood gazing out upon the river, over the glittering waters of which, skiff, wherry and other craft still glided. "It is such a treat after night after night of boards and footlights, to get once in a way into the fresh air. Evenings like this are rarities with me."

"I suppose so, yet you love your profession and the applause that greets your successes."

"Yes, indeed! hard work as it is at times, I am fond of it now. It is a career dear to most of us who succeed. There are few other phases in life where woman tastes more frequently the sweets of gratified vanity."

"And you are not above owning that weakness?"

"No," laughed the actress, "it is in me strong, I fear; and, moreover, Mr. Merrington, take my word for it you'll find it, a little more or a little less, not varying very much either, in every woman you will ever meet, and if I add in every man also, I shall not be far out."

Here they were interrupted by Thorndale. "About time to make tracks, I reckon," observed that gentleman, as he sauntered up to them. "Brazeley's ordered his *fiacre*. Guess I'd best do the same. Can I be of any use to you and Mrs. Crosse, Miss Jerningham, about getting back to town?"

"No, thanks, we've a carriage of our own."

"Well, I've two seats to spare if any one wants a ride."

Seth Thorndale could talk very fair English when he chose; but with that extreme self-assertion that constitutes rather a weak point in the American character, he preferred as a rule to interlard his converse with Americanisms. It was a sort of protest against the old country generally that relieved his mind.

Fortie saw Lizzie and her *chaperon* to their brougham. He lingered a moment at the carriage window as he said good-bye to Lizzie, and expressed a hope he should shortly see her again.

"Depends more upon you than me, Mr. Merrington," laughed the actress. "You see you have confessedly nothing to do, and I have lots; but I trust we shall meet again ere long."

"Now, Fortie, my chick, get your coat and come away," exclaimed Furnival. "You're all ready, ain't you, Jim?"

"Been good for a start the last hour, myself. Did my *devoir* to Mrs. Basinghall, and felt rather exhausted in the process. She was a good-looking woman, but that's were it is, she *was*."

"Pleasant to talk to though, now. Well, Fortie, my boy, have you enjoyed your day? Have the fairy birds been singing? You had a good deal of Lizzie Jerningham to yourself, and she can make things *couleur de rose* when she's so minded, and it must have been your fault if she was not."

"Yes, thanks to you, I have put in a very pleasant evening."

"Don't know about my having much to say to it. Should fancy if you asked them, Basinghall or Lizzie would take credit to themselves upon that subject. Though, perhaps, if you go back to first causes, I was the source from which your gratification sprang."

Ere they separated, Fortie had accepted an invitation to dinner from Halden. An evil augury. Jim Halden was not addicted to playing the amphytrion, and his dinners boded little good to his guests.

CHAPTER VII.

THE CURATE'S NEWS.

ST. HELENS is fair to look upon these pleasant summer days when,

> "Midsummer, like an army with banners, is moving through the heavens."

Things trickle along so gently in these quiet out of the way country places, that existence dwindles almost to a monotone. It is curious how, by a merciful law of Nature, the mind contracts under these circumstances, how we arrive gradually at an interest in the health of our neighbour's turkeys, still more intensified at the intelligence that his potatoes are struck with blight. Men fret a good deal when they first commence this sort of life, after having been accustomed to more exciting scenes. But if they have passed the first flush of manhood, they soon acquire such minor interests as I have mentioned. The tranquillity soothes them : they become lotos eaters, and shrink from anything that may disturb the calm easiness of existence. To the very young such solitude is a blight; sympathy and selfishness are the fundamental principles of the human mind, say the philosophers. To eliminate the former is to inculcate the latter. But to those who have stemmed the shock of life's fierce torrent, it is a relief.

Kate Moseley had not as yet settled down to the dull monotony of her home life. If she had been but a school girl before, it had been on an advanced scale. The *pension* to which she was attached was of a very liberal and enlightened type; the elder girls were taken about to see most of the great sights of Paris, such as the Louvre, &c. She had, too, dear friends of her own age, and of her own intellectual culture to associate with. After the first excitement of her return home, that home speedily palled upon her. Then came the meeting with Fortie, and that pleasant flirtation which had added more zest to existence than Katie was quite aware of at the time. His departure did him good service, for while he, immersed in the whirl of London life only occasionally thought about her, Kate brooded a good deal over those pleasant wanderings by the river.

She was rather a coquette, and for sheer lack of employment had of late tried her hand on the Reverend Phillip Filander, whom she was gradually reducing to a state of extreme prostration. Of course, with plenty of resources within herself she had no business to have felt bored, *distrait*, *ennuyé;* but however great our resources in our nineteenth year, we yearn for sympathy in our pursuits.

She had coaxed her father once or twice

into taking her up with him to the Manor House, and she had made good use of those opportunities. She had exerted all her powers to charm on Sir Giles, and the old cynic was pleased with her fair young face, fresh ideas, shrewd remarks, and clever deference to himself. She had extorted permission to visit the library when she chose, pleading the dearth of books in her father's house. But she began now to wish Fortic would return. She liked him better than she thought she had done, and Kate began to ponder whether marriage were not possible between the two. She was far too clever not to see all the difficulties of the situation. Sir Giles might smile at their flirtation, but his wrath would be at hurricane pitch should they murmur matrimony. Then she thought of Mrs. De Driby, and Kate laughed a saucy little laugh, as she thought of that lady's face if the time should ever come when she should address her as dear aunt.

Miss Moseley has not got over Mrs. De Driby's contemptuous treatment of her pretty self on the occasion of Sir Giles's dinner, and two or three similar passages have added fuel to the flames of her indignation. How women do hate each other under these circumstances. What vengeance will they not cherish in their hearts, and with what virulence will they not mete it out to the offender when the hour comes.

Kate this spring evening is toying with some feminine frivolities at a little table on the close-shaven lawn by the streamlet's bank. Pretty enough picture she makes, with her golden hair and light diaphanous draperies, and so thinks the Reverend Phillip Filander, as he makes his way across the soft grass to pay his now almost daily visit.

I have not as yet said much about the curate, the type is very common-place. There are so many men imbued with vanity and bashfulness. He was a good little man at bottom, but in his secret soul he cherished two beliefs. One that he possessed within him pulpit eloquence of no mean ability; the other that he was an omnipotent power with regard to womankind. These opinions were theoretical in the extreme, a more harmless Don Juan could not have existed, even had not the curate's character completely precluded his aspiring to anything worse than mild flirtation. Women are wont wonderfully to strengthen a man of this type in his belief. It is extraordinary the compassion they feel for shyness in the male creature—they are tender with him, and draw him out and make much of him from sheer pity at his shamefacedness. What wonder that the man sometimes mistakes their motives, and attributes their kindness to the result of his own fascinations. For vanity, bear it in mind, is a very component part in shyness. It is connected a good deal, especially in the male sex, with the fear of not being appraised at the value we place upon ourselves. A shy curate in particular is wont to be much taken care of by the fair members of his flock. Phillip Filander thoroughly believed in his success, as he would have expressed it, with the ladies. Look at the slippers, sermon-cases, watch-guards, &c., which attested the triumph of the conqueror.

Regarding his pulpit eloquence, he composed little oratorical effects into which he emptied the slight knowledge acquired in his Oxford days — stuttered them forth to an agricultural congregation who slept quietly through his classical allusions. Whether his sermons were good or bad, his unfortunate hesitating delivery precluded all possibility of judging. The greater discourses of the greatest divines must have fallen flat filtered through such a feeble channel. Why is not committing to memory as much compulsory in the pulpit as on the stage? Can a preacher who stumbles about his manuscript ever arrest the attention of a congregation? Do not the great readers of the day invariably know their readings by heart? The book is a mere accessory, they glance at it for effect but not for information.

Kate, to divert the monotony of her existence, has entangled the curate in a mild flirtation; but I wot that is little likely to disturb Miss Moseley's peace of mind. With her great sympathetic power, she is likely to be dangerous many times to men before she is meshed herself. Yet, come the time soon or come it late, Kate is of that nature that loves once and for ever. Such women marry or do not marry the love of their heart, but it lingers with them to the death. The last kiss may be with the husband, but the last thought is with that one lost love.

But all this time the curate has been advancing, and now taking off his hat wishes Miss Moseley "good day."

Kate extends her little hand as she

says, "Delighted to see you, Mr. Filander, though it's but a poor compliment; for truth to say I was getting so bored with embroidery that any interruption would have been welcome."

"Charmed I'm sure to think that, that, I should be of such es-essential service."

Mr. Filander had no real stammer, it was simply shyness that made him falter in his speech.

"Well," smiled Kate, "what have you been doing with yourself this delicious day? I have just received an invitation from the Stephensons to a croquet party for Tuesday next. I suppose you are going."

"Yes, I think so, that is I said I would."

"Of course you are. There is so little doing in this quiet place, that anything of the kind which brings us in contact with our fellow-creatures is a relief."

"Yes," replied the curate, getting more at his ease. "Their parties are always pleasant, so I suppose I shall go."

A great weakness of mankind, "supposing they will go," when they have already quite made up their minds on the subject. But it does not do to hold oneself too cheap, so as a salve to our vanity we express ourselves thus, the thing might do as a *dernière ressource.* The infirmity is by no means confined to the provinces, and is exemplified quite as often in a London season.

"A Mrs. Briarly I hear is to be there; who is she? I never heard of her before."

"Well, I never met her, but I hear she is the widow of a squire of the neighbourhood who died under, under rather exceptional circumstances nearly two years ago."

A delicate way of explaining that a series of experiments in strong drinks on a weak constitution had resulted in a premature grave.

"Mrs. De Driby and the Rector,

I presume, will be of the party?"

"Ye—yes, and I d—did hear something about Sir Giles. Mr. De Driby seems rather in a way about about Mr. Merrington."

"Why, what of him?" inquired Kate, sharply.

"He didn't say much, but he hinted or seemed to th—th—think that he was not going on well in town. I don't know what, b—b—but I believe his father was very wild, and Mr. Merrington takes after him."

"I never heard that because a man's father was guilty of serious crimes," replied Miss Moseley, "that it was a necessity or law of nature that his son also should be addicted to the same."

Mr. Filander was a little startled at the acerbity of Kate's manner, and meekly deprecated such opinion, although he said that it was so in the more modified form of wildness of disposition at times, and that he feared Mr. Merrington had got into some trouble.

But this also Katie laughed somewhat to scorn, and the curate found Miss Moseley much less kind to him than usual. He lingered on a little, but the rumour he had brought regarding Fortie had set Katie thinking. She was *distrait* and absent, and sooth to say a little waspish at last with him. She longed to be alone, and it was with feelings of considerable satisfaction that she at last saw the curate take his departure.

When he was gone, Katie rested her head upon her hand and began to think—she thought first whether she really cared for Fortie Merrington. No, she liked him and should be most sincerely sorry for him if he had got into a scrape of any kind, no more than that; then she thought of what little she had heard her father tell relating to Sefton Merrington. Not much, but wild stories they were, as far as she recollected. From her knowledge of Fortie's unstable disposition, she could but admit that Filander had fair grounds for his assumption, although she had utterly refused to recognise such reasoning from his lips. Then she thought what if she went up to the Manor House, she might probably see Sir Giles and perchance hear something more authentic from him concerning Fortie's misdoings.

Katie caught up her hat, and tripped lightly along the bank of the stream. She wondered whether Fortie was really in trouble, then she thought of all those pleasant strolls along that very path with him only some two months or so ago, when he affected to fish and she to sketch. Pleasant they were though neither of them did much in their pretended callings. Katie's knowledge of the world was as yet circumscribed, and derived principally from works of fiction. Despite her French training, she had imbibed as yet but little of Balzac, and was innocent of George Sand, two writers that expand the mind a good deal at eighteen, though whether in the right direction is perhaps liable to question. She felt instinctively that Horace disliked his cousin, and was not likely to gloss over any story to his disadvantage.

Full of such thoughts, she arrived at the Manor House. The servants were used to her flitting visits there now. "Scandalous," Mrs. De Driby had termed them, when they first came to her ears; but happening to make that remark to her brother-in-law, he had quietly replied: "Nonsense, the girl is well enough, let her alone, Louisa. If she likes to tumble over the old books, she may as far as I am concerned."

Katie just asked if Sir Giles was in, and on receiving the reply "he thought not," from the footman, made her way to the old library without further inquiry.

Once there, she soon hunted out a

book, and sat down to look it over a little before she returned home. But it would not do, she was still thinking of Fortie, and what scrape he might have got into, or whether he had got into a scrape at all. It might be mere spiteful prediction on Mr. De Driby's part. Well she must go now, so she tied up her two volumes of Elizabeth Browning, put on her hat and started; ere she had got twenty yards from the house she met Sir Giles.

"Plundering the old library again, I see Miss Moseley," said the Baronet, as he raised his hat. "Not a vice the young ladies of the present day are addicted to."

"I suppose, Sir Giles, they read as much as their grandmothers did," retorted Kate.

"Yes, a little more; they read all the proceedings of the Divorce Court, and most of the French novels. They don't condescend much to the English, unless accredited as very highly spiced."

"In the name of my sex, I cry libel, rank heretical libel, Sir Giles. Are you not afraid of prosecution."

"I should be—no libel incurs such heavy penalties as truth; the enunciators of that have paid dear for their whistle time out of mind."

"Ah, that's the way you always evade me. No; women are not all of the type you would lead one to suppose. Some of them still read sensible books, and lead sensible lives."

"Egad!" laughed the Baronet, "they're like the honest man of Diogenes then, a little difficult to meet with. I don't know that they're worse than the men though."

"Ah! talking of the men, when's Mr. Merrington coming down again?"

"Weugh!" whistled the Baronet, "sets the wind in that quarter."

"No," said Katie, as her cheeks flushed, and her eyes sparkled, "the wind does not set in that quarter. If I can't make a common inquiry of courtesy without being misconstrued, I'll wish you 'good evening,' Sir Giles. I could have fancied Mrs. De Driby making such a remark, but not you," and Kate, drawing her small self to her full height, was about to depart in her wrath.

"Stop, Miss Moseley," said the Baronet, and his half jesting tones became frigid as he spoke. "I was never yet accused of discourtesy to a lady. I should have thought what an old man like myself might say to a girl like you, should be viewed in a different light from that in which it might appear coming from a lady. In my day, a maxim much inculcated was, that loss of temper was loss of manners."

"Ah, Sir Giles, I beg your pardon; but you must own Mrs. De Driby has a bitter tongue of her own. She has made me sensitive on many points on which I have no call to be. You must forgive me, if I got angry without cause."

Katie was a little hypocritical after the manner of women on such subjects.

"Yes, I can fancy Louisa has said sharp things to you. You come from her own class. No people are so spiteful to the class just below them, as those who have just emerged from it. But when people are quite assured of their station, Miss Moseley, they don't commit such *bêtises*. However, I see you forgive me Fortie was very well when I heard last from him, so now good-night," and the Baronet stalked away. When he talked of never having been discourteous to woman, he believed he spoke the truth. He was quite unconscious of the extreme impertinence conveyed in his last speech. On the contrary, he thought he had behaved with all the stately politeness of that old school he so much affected.

As for Kate, she ground her little white

teeth as she muttered, "Yes, you can be as rude in your way as your sister-in-law. These aristocrats, they don't think we're the same clay as themselves. *Va*, the time will come perhaps when you De Dribys will think differently."

Katie had imbibed strong republican ideas in her scholastic career at Paris. Her most intimate friend at the *pension* had been an American girl, called Zare Harland. Zare was democratic to the tips of her pretty fingers, and had, in the end, embued Kate with a strong dash of her own opinions on these points. With her little head full of such thoughts Katie returned home.

"Well, girl!" said her father, as she entered. Ye've been up to the big house for books, I s'pose. Did ye see aught of Sir Giles?"

"Yes, I saw him just as I came away. How proud he is, father!"

"Aye, child, they ever were; they're fell as they're proud too, the whole race.

They never forgive them as crosses 'em. I mind his father with poor Steve Fosberry, the time he angered him about the shooting. Poor Steve and his family had been on the farm for generations, but Sir Ralph said go he should, and go he did. He offered more rent and pleaded hard to be allowed to stop in the old place he had been born in; but it was no use. I think I see Sir Ralph now, as he said in his cold gibing way. 'No, my man, there's but two things left I'll do for you; as an old tenant, I'll give you an elm tree when your time comes, and let you six feet by three of the estate on perpetual lease.'"

"Oh, father, did he say that?"

"Yes, my lass, and meant it. Sir Giles aint a deal better either. Dear, it seems but yesterday that Squire Cunliffe crossed him about that right of way. I recollect when the magistrates gave it against him, Sir Giles said in his grim way, 'Ah, Mr. Cunliffe, you don't know the expense of road making yet; but you will before you die.' He did, poor man, for it ruined him clean. Sir Giles brought action after action against him, they moved from court to court, and when the right was finally decided in Cunliffe's favour, he'd about spent all he had in law. I don't know how much it cost Sir Giles; but what did he care, he had broken Cunliffe, and I don't think he troubled his head much about the roadway after. But didn't I hear ye say, Kate, ye'd an invite to go and see these Stephenson people."

"Yes, father, and you too. You don't suppose I would go unless you were invited?"

"Eh, girl, that's all very well. You're good to think of the old father in a way too. But it won't work. When ye've passed your life at the plough ye don't run handy in the carriage. They mean kindly, but ye must learn to gad about by yerself, lass. I'm over old for junketting, much more for quality frisks."

"But, father, you must go too, or else I shall not."

"Tut, tut, child, leave the old man to go his own way; but I'll have you go. It's dulsome like for a bright young thing like you, this lonely life. And mind, Katie, I'll have you dressed with the best. I know naught about such things myself; but see you've silks, satins, and such like fripperies with the best of 'em. I've plenty to rig my little girl out in anything she fancies. I've made a bit of money in my time, and I've only you to think of, child."

"I know, father dear, I can always have what I like in that way, but I want you to come with me."

"And I tell you, I won't—and I won't have you stay to home neither. Ye must learn to go about by yourself, lass. It can't be helped. I want you to mix with all these fine folk, as ye're fit for. Ye looked better nor any of them that time at the Manor House. I'll always find the brass, girl — there's a bit in the bank."

"But why won't you come, father?"

"Don't argue, child; but do as you're bid. A steer's a good beast in its way, but it don't look its best in a flower-garden. I'll stay home, and you shall tell me all about it afterwards."

Birkett Moseley loved his daughter very dearly, and was extremely solicitous she should settle well in life. He had brought her up as a lady, and wished to see her become one *de facto* by marriage. His strong natural sense told him that her sphere was not that which he had been brought up in. When he saw how much she was made of that night at the Manor House, he rapidly resolved that he would never be a drag upon her getting into any society. With his keen penetration, he saw that people would welcome the pretty brilliant educated girl, who would shrink from the rough unpolished father. His love was great, and witnessing Kate's little social triumph that evening had been very sweet to him.

CHAPTER VIII.

A SOCIAL SPIDER.

SEATED in his study, Horace De Driby was musing over many things. He reflected with bitterness over the cold welcome he had received from Sir Giles but yesterday, and with what interest he had spoken of Fortie. He thought vindictively over the idea of three-parts of that rich inheritance, which he had been brought up to regard as his own, being alienated from him. His strong sombre mind had pondered much over this of late, and the more he pondered the more did his naturally fierce nature resent what he deemed the injustice that threatened him. It is true he was in utter ignorance of Sir Giles's real intentions, and that after all he might not like to separate the property from the baronetcy. The pride of race was equally strong both in uncle and nephew. No De Driby had ever done so before, but then this was the first instance in which there had not been a direct descendant.

Then his thoughts finally settled down upon what his town correspondence had brought him anent Fortie and his doings. He had dropped no hint the day before to Sir Giles of what he had heard, his acute penetration had told him that Fortie must commit himself first in his uncle's eyes without his intervention, but once let that happen, as he felt it surely would, and it should be his care to see the breach never closed. The sore on both sides should never heal. Let him alone to produce gangrene in the wounds.

His dark eyes glittered, as he muttered: "So the young fool has taken the first step without my moving a finger. Clayton, who writes me this, knows the Babylonish life in all its phases. I should think I might rely upon his information. Nevertheless, I think it's worth running up to town to see about. I've a business man too, that I paid pretty dearly for making the acquaintance of in my younger days, that it might be worth while to look up again. He could be useful in certain changes of my game, and could always obtain me the most reliable information about Fortie's pecuniary affairs. For money too, I should think there're be little he'd stick at. Mere question of how much."

So Horace determined that he would proceed to London by the afternoon train, and entering the drawing-room apprised his mother of his intention, and then taking his hat started for the lodgings of the Reverend Mr. Filander, to tell him he must prepare himself to perform the whole of next Sunday's duties.

That gentleman was not a little perturbed, and stuttered out, "but my dear sir, I've not quite pre—prepared my own sermon, and this you know is Fri—Fri—Friday. So little time you see to get re—ready a second."

"You can preach one of the old ones over again," retorted the Rector, sententiously, "the agricultural mind is slow to receive, and I daresay has not yet thoroughly mastered any of your discourses. Any way, I must go, so do the best you can."

"What can take you to town, my dear Horace, in this abrupt manner!" exclaimed Mrs. De Driby, on his return. "I'm sure, considering the short stay my health admits of my making in this part of the country, it's very inconsiderate, to say the least of it, to leave me all by myself."

"It's only for three nights, mother, I shall be back on Monday, and with your intellectual resources, what might be dull to another woman will not affect you."

"Ah, yes, my dear, I shall have to live within myself as of old," replied Mrs. De Driby, intensely mollified by this Jesuitical remark. "If it was not for the duties that society exacts from people of our station, I could with pleasure resign myself to a solitary life in the great world of intellect. To wander through the play of Shakespeare's fancy, the majestic thoughts of Bacon, the polished accuracy of Hume, the sweet imaginings of Shelley, the sublimity of Milton, the, the—in short, my dear boy, to a life of intellect."

Mrs. Horace quoted her authors pretty glibly. She was by no means the first woman, who has assumed reading the title pages in a library constitutes a liberal education. Her son was most thoroughly conversant with his mother's weaknesses, yet on the one point of the family pride and his right to the entire inheritance, he was as complete a convert as she could have wished.

Self-interest sometimes blinds men's eyes

to truth. Keen sighted on every other point, Horace De Driby never recognised that his uncle had already provided for him, and had further the right to do what he liked with his own On this point he was smitten with mental obliquity. He saw only an uncle meditating a deadly wrong to himself, and a scapegrace boy on the watch to take advantage of it. That Sir Giles had as yet not contemplated the time when he must resign the lands of St. Helens and all other possessions in this world on the one hand, and that what would be the result when he did, had never crossed Fortie Merrington's volatile mind on the other, never entered into his calculations. He had enunciated the maxim that he and Fortie, from their social position, must be foes. He looked upon Sir Giles as the monarch waxing old, for whose sceptre they were bound to struggle, and Horace De Driby with the family thirst for aggrandisement strong on him, vowed Fortie should be never a penny the better for his uncle's death.

These strong tenacious minds, when they once grasp a belief of this kind, incorporate it with their very being. The law courts are prolific in such instances. In them, rights of way, and rights of water-courses have been battled for as fiercely, aye, and died for as grimly, as three centuries ago they had been on blood-stained fields. Has not Mr. Dickens given us the immortal picture of "the man from Shropshire." Do we not all know that his prototype exists and will exist till "the wicked cease from troubling, and the weary are at peace." Under these circumstances, in the old days, you slew your adversary in fair fight if you could. As the age advanced, you paid other people to perform that sometimes dangerous service for you. In these days, uncultivated minds mostly prefer poison; but the higher and more intellectual class rely principally upon social calumny. It is a tolerably deadly poison in the hands of an unscrupulous enemy, and verily, my brethren, your path must have been straight and virtuous through life, if a good hater with no regard to veracity cannot envenom the life blood of your social system.

In one of those dark gloomy little streets that run from the East Strand to the river, dwelt Mr. Richard Phinny, attorney-at-law. The ground floor of the house was fitted up as offices, over them lived Phinny and his brood. On the ground floor, with the assistance of a couple of clerks, Phinny pursued his vocation of a social spider. Above, Mrs. Phinny and her daughters gave themselves up to the all absorbing phantom-chase of what they termed gentility, that is in genuine English the aping of their betters. Mr. Phinny, in his web-like gloomy offices, sucked weekly the blood of divers social butterflies for the benefit of his ambitious belongings upstairs. A stout oily man with an unctuous voice, a low chuckling laugh, and a habit of constantly washing his hands when he spoke to you. His practice lay a good deal in the discounting line. Few of the usurers of London but whom were well acquainted with Mr. Phinny. Whether acting in their behalf, or trying to smooth the difficulties of some sanguine, youthful, and reckless signer of stamped paper, the attorney contrived to invariably get a good pull at somebody's quill feathers. Most of his clients, as he wished them an unctuous farewell, entered into the feelings of a Lincolnshire goose after plucking time. The world was wont to look hard and cold, as it doubtless does to those despoiled innocents of the fen country.

Mr. Phinny would probably in confidence have told you that feathers must be had, that social geese are as much a law of creation as their ornithological brethren, and that he was no crueller than the Lincolnshire housewife. In one sense he was; opportunity serving, he was apt to pluck with ungenerous closeness, insomuch that some of the social geese that passed through his hands never arrived at anything like full plumage again during their life time.

It was down this street, a short time after his arrival in town, that the Rev. Horace De Driby might have been descried making his way. He walked like a man in no uncertainty about his destination, and turned through the little outer door like a man conversant with Phinny's offices, as, in truth, he had been at one period of his life.

Yes, the Rev. Horace in his time had gone through the process of a compulsory moulting in that grimy little den, and that so little to his own satisfaction, that he could hardly repress a slight shudder as he inquired of one of the clerks if Mr. Phinny was within. The reply was in the affirmative, and he was at once ushered into that inner sanctuary, which one of the initiated had once described as the entrance to the everlasting sea of accumulative debt.

"Dear, dear, Mr. De Driby, to think of the many years it is since I've had the pleasure of seeing you!" exclaimed the presiding deity (there are deities for evil as well as for good in this world, and, perchance, the former have the more worshippers of the two). He spoke in those strong unctuous tones, that imply an invitation to a glass of brown sherry and a biscuit must be the first proposition of their owner. "Yes, it seems a long time since I last had the honour of seeing you. But you look well, sir, you look well; the destroyer has dealt leniently with you. Pray be seated. You have been saved the wear and tear of business, it is likely. How I envy you. As for me, you find me at the collar as before, like the old mill horse, Mr. De Driby, doomed to travel his petty circle, and drop in harness at last."

"The world don't seem to have used

you badly," replied Horace. "You look much as I remember you some years ago."

"You flatter me—yes, sir, flatter me. It's kind of you to say so; but the constant work begins to tell. I feel it, not but what I am equal to it as yet. My clients don't find their interests suffer, I think, in my hands. But might I inquire in what way I can be useful? Time, unfortunately, you see, is money to us professional people."

"I shan't detain you long. I presume, if it is made worth your while, you could speedily ascertain pretty nearly how much paper any young man in town has afloat?"

"Hum, yes. I should fancy so, in a few days. There would be expenses to incur, you are, of course, aware. Any one you are interested in?"

"Of course I am, or I shouldn't take the trouble to see about it"

"Would it be too much to inquire in

what way you are interested on the subject?"

"Yes. Take my instructions or not, as you please; but don't ask superfluous questions."

"Pardon, Mr. De Driby. I have no intention of doing so. But allow me to make one observation. When you do see a solicitor, it is best to make a clean breast of it to him. I have made that remark a good many times, Mr. De Driby," continued the attorney, washing his hands and addressing an imaginary audience over Horace's head, "though I can't call to mind that anybody ever benefitted much by it. But, dear me, the scores of fine young men who have done me the honour to consult me, and rendered my efforts unavailing through these half confidences."

"It's no young man in your sense of the phrase who has come to see you now. Secondly, I have not come to consult, but to direct."

"Forgive me, my dear sir, I was only speaking for the best, I assure you."

"It will save a deal of time, Mr. Phinny, if you will thoroughly understand, that the man who now speaks to you, is very different from the inexperienced collegian you remember. I apply to you, simply as I consider you the easiest channel for acquiring the information it is my whim or business to procure. Do you understand me?"

"Certainly! my dear sir, certainly!" replied the attorney, again washing his hands, though with considerably less assurance, than he had shown at the commencement of the interview.

"Good? then in eight-and-forty hours I must know how far Mr. Fortescue Merrington is involved with the Jews, or whether he is not involved at all. I must further know, as much as you can pick up in the time, with regard to his general liabilities, debts to tradesmen, debts of honour, &c. You've made a note of the name I see, that's his address. I have nothing more to add, further than that you will call upon me on Monday morning with such information as you have acquired at Cox's Hotel in Jermyn Street."

"I will do my best. Your instructions Mr. De Driby, if not confidential, are—he—he—short and explicit."

"I see no further necessity for explanation, Mr. Phinny. If your instructions are not quite clear, perhaps you will say so."

"Perfectly! perfectly! my dear sir. How I wish all my clients were anything like as lucid as you are."

"Good day then," and Horace rose, resumed his hat and passed out.

"Good day, good day, my dear sir. Slack," he cried, to one of his clerks, as the door closed on the Rector, "just bring me the ledgers of '55 and '56, I want to look through them. I think I'll just look through our former relations a bit. I must understand this business a little better—I've known a simple inquiry turn out very profitable in my time; people will sometimes pay considerably sooner than it should be known they have made it, harmless though it may be;" with which remark Mr. Phinny betook himself to a severe study of the back ledgers.

Monday brought the Rector but little information, that is what he deemed useful information. The attorney reported that as far as he could make out, Fortescue Merrington's name was as yet unknown to the tribes, that he could learn nothing about any liabilities he had incurred of any consequence, that he lived in a fastish set; but that there was one fact to make him uneasy if he took an interest in Mr. Merrington—"

"And that is?" inquired Horace.

"His intimacy, sir, with the Honourable James Halden; that young man has brought a good many of his intimates into trouble. His own acceptance is not worth the stamp it is written on. Perfectly aware of that fact he, as far as he can, persuades his friends to write their names for his benefit, and has been unusually successful so far."

"Ah! thank you, that will do for the present. But you will remember, Mr. Phinny, to keep your eye on this case, please." Horace spoke as indifferently as if he were exhorting a subordinate to attend to a rather curious case in natural history that had lately come under his notice.

The attorney retired, well satisfied with the douceur that had rewarded his researches, but completely in the dark as to what motive his employer could have in such inquiries. "Never mind," he muttered to himself, "when it's worth a man's while to know about the proceedings of a young gentleman like this, it's likely to be a long surveillance, and it will go hard if I don't know 'the why' before my turn of detective is over."

CHAPTER IX.

THE ANATOMY OF CROQUET.

HORACE DE DRIBY returned to St. Helens in ample time to escort his mother to the Stephensons' croquet party. That estimable lady looked forward to doing a good deal in the patronizing way, a *rôle* she dearly loved, on the occasion. She therefore welcomed the avatar of a fine day with condescending approbation.

"I'm really quite glad, my dear," she observed to her son at breakfast, "that the Stephensons have got such charming weather for their party. It is so hard on little folks in the country, when they have been exerting themselves to the utmost for days past, to be thwarted by the capriciousness of our climate. Women in poor Mrs. Stephenson's position naturally feel failure in these entertainments so much. She is such a nice unassuming person, that I should have felt it a duty—yes, quite a duty, my dear Horace, to have shown there for a few minutes almost under any circumstances."

I regret to say that these miserable Stephensons, utterly unconscious of the honour about to be conferred upon them, were not the least perplexed about these arrangements, but certainly a little perturbed at the unfortunate circumstance of Mrs. De Driby's acceptance of their invitation.

"Such a bore for you, dear mamma," said Isabel, the eldest. "You'll have to talk to her all the afternoon. We couldn't help asking her, but who would have thought she would come?"

Gorgeous in silk, lace, and parasol, did Mrs. De Driby sweep up the Stephensons' lawn, already studded with a little knot of croquet enthusiasts sending the red through the hoop, and the adverse black into solitude and sulkiness in the adjacent shrubberies. There was Mrs. Briarly, a bold dark-eyed buxom widow in slight mourning, looking as if she had borne the loss of the dear departed very fairly, and having evident intentions of providing herself with a substitute ere the year was over. At present she was apparently employed in the subjugation of the Reverend Phillip Filander. There were the Stephenson girls dressed in neat costume and Spanish hats; there was Kate Moseley in the light muslin draperies, coquettish straw hat and pale blue ribbons she so much affected; and last, though not least, Sir Giles, talking to Mr. Stephenson, was looking on at the fray.

"So charmed, so delighted to see you, my dear Mrs. Stephenson!" exclaimed Mrs. De Driby, taking her hostess's hands in both her own, (it was her notion of affability.) "So fortunate in your weather too. What, Giles, you here? I had no idea you were a votary of croquet. Ah, we live and learn, Mrs. Stephenson!"

"Doubtful in some cases, Louisa—certainly not as a rule."

"Ah, you are laughing at me because I don't understand it."

"Not the least. Very few of the players do. It's the finest anatomist of character I have contemplated for some time. Give the game time, and it will dissect the minds of all these people who think they are merely knocking balls through hoops."

"I don't quite follow you, Giles."

"Of course you don't, because you don't follow the game. Sit down here and watch it attentively for half an hour, and then compare your opinion with mine."

A grim smile flitted across Sir Giles' face as his sister-in-law prepared deliberately to follow his suggestion.

At this juncture, one of the young lady

players who had just been roquèd with uncalled for severity from the other end of the lawn to nearly where Sir Giles and Mr. Stephenson were standing, exclaiming, "Oh, what a shame!" rushed across in pursuit of her ball.

"There, Stephenson!" exclaimed the Baronet, "a case in point. Women were not intended to run. Nothing justifies a woman in running but the threatened loss of her life or her lover. Specimen of irrepressible womanhood that."

The game proceeded, showing forth, as the Baronet predicted, much bitterness and anguish of spirit. Equable temperament, and steady nerve had their victory as they do usually on the greater battle-fields of life. The conquerors crowed over the vanquished after the immutable law of nature. *Væ victis* was, as of old, the predominant cry, and the beaten in the tournay bore the scoffs of the victors with as little patience as they do in larger matters. The triumph of the one party is vexation to the other through life generally. The genial winner must produce the discomfited loser. We can't all have even the sugar plums we play for, and are wont inwardly to weep over these lost *confitures*, much as we did in the days of our childhood; we think we have attained stoicism when we no longer bore our friends with our plaints.

"There, Louisa," whispered the Baronet, as a fresh game having commenced Isabel Stephenson roquèd Mrs. Briarly's ball far away to the extremity of the ground, "do you see that? Can you translate?—that means Mrs. Briarly has monopolized the Curate considerably more than seems right in Miss Stephenson's eyes, she don't care a rush about separating their balls; but she don't mean to stand that *tête-à-tête* any longer."

It suited Sir Giles' cynic temperament to reduce the game to a metaphysical problem. "Clever, that," he remarked.

"You don't suppose Mr. Gilmour meant to roquè that ball, it might be *the* game, but it was not his game; how cleverly he missed and has dropped himself down within a couple of yards of your daughter Jenny. Not a bad player that young gentleman, whatever people may say of him."

An elderly young lady here came up to Mr. Stephenson, and in answer to his inquiry of how she was getting on, replied, "Oh, shockingly! I can't get any one to help me through my hoops."

"They never can, Stephenson, at that age;" chuckled Sir Giles, as the young lady betook herself once more to her ball. "She has no more right to expect to be helped through her hoops than on with a ring."

"Why, you don't suppose, Sir Giles, that people really play croquet with all these far-fetched schemes that you, in the bitterness of your humour, are just now pleased to attribute to them."

"My dear Stephenson," replied the

Baronet, in that bland manner with which he was wont to make his most acrid observations. "I don't mix much in the world now, but I have in my day. I fancy I am a very tolerable judge of life's counters as used in society. You may think that invitations mean simply hospitality, that the ball-room means sociability, enjoyment, and dancing. Pshaw! men and women are gambling for hearts, and speculating on social advancement. A dinner party is often a hard-fought field—not a ball but produces its *Io triumphè* to some, the fatal *væ victis* to others. I know nothing that affords greater scope than croquet for clever manœuvring of this sort."

"Well, Sir Giles; it's my belief that four-fifths of the people who play it, do so heartily from mere love of the game and for sheer amusement; however, I see there's something in the eating and drinking way going on. I am afraid it's useless asking you to join our nondescript meal, but come and have a glass of wine at all events. I will guarantee my sherry sound and honest."

"I'll just say good-bye to Mrs. Stephenson, and then I must be going; I hate being out after sunset now, and regard evening dews with horror and dismay."

Mrs. De Driby was, as may be imagined, a sight to see throughout the day. She patronized meek Mrs. Stephenson, till the daughters of that estimable lady simmered with wrath, while Kate Moseley bubbled over with wickedness. She levelled her gold eye-glass, with what she deemed aristocratic condescension, on the baser clay it was her lot to mix with.

"Does you great credit, Mrs. Stephenson, indeed, quite an elegant collation. How you and your dear girls manage it, I'm sure I can't imagine. But thanks to your bringing up, they know how to be useful as well as look nice, after household cares have been attended to;" and here Mrs. De Driby smiled urbanely, feeling that she had been sweetly complimentary.

"What an affected piece of impertinence she is," whispered Isabel Stephenson to Kate, "how I should like to shake her. I don't mean to say that Jennie and I haven't done our best to make our table look pretty, but we don't want to be reminded of our labours in that way. Mrs. De Driby would insinuate that we have done all the cooking."

"And what harm if you had, Isabel?" retorted Kate. "I'm a nobody, and therefore it don't much matter what I think; but if I wanted my party to go off well, I should not mind what work I lent my hand to beforehand. It's little I'd reck of what the Mrs. De Driby's of this world might say on the subject."

"Thanks, Katie;" replied Miss Stephenson, "but take care, your own turn will come ere long."

"How unkind of you to frighten me; I can only hope I may prove equal to the occasion when it does," replied Kate, demurely.

Isabel Stephenson looked curiously at her neighbour for a minute, and then said, "I should not wonder if you did, and to say the honest truth I should rather like to see you tried."

"Mr. Filander!" exclaimed Kate, as the curate made his way into her vicinity, "I wonder you dare venture near me, after the scandalous manner you have neglected me all day; are you not afraid the pent up torrent of my indignation may overwhelm you?"

"I'm sure, Miss Moseley, it was not from want of inclination, but—b-b-b-but you see," stuttered the curate, "Mrs. Briarly not understanding the game, she required so much instruction."

"And so you smoothed the stony places for her, did you? Metamorphosed the rude iron hoops into golden circlets; beware of such alchemy, Mr. Filander—transmuted the cage of rancour and despair into a bower of roses—again, I say, take heed, Mr. Filander."

The curate coloured in confusion at Kate's merciless attack; but aid arrived from an unforeseen quarter. Mrs. De Driby was making her way down the room, her carriage having been announced. She paused to say good night to the Stephenson girls. "Ah, Miss Moseley," she exclaimed, "I dare say you have found out by this time the sad mistake your father made in sending you to that absurd French school. Quite unfitted you for a country life, no doubt?"

"Not at all; come and try, Mrs. De Driby. We will give you some croquet any day you like to name next week, and if I can't make as good a syllabub as ever you tasted, then you shall say my French schooling was a mistake."

Mrs. De Driby's face was a sight to see, as Kate, with a pleasant smile, gave her off-hand invitation. The idea that a chit of a farmer's daughter, to whom she looked upon it as a condescension on her part to speak, should presume to ask her, Mrs. De Driby, to croquet and syllabub, literally took away her breath. She recovered herself with a violent effort, and like a true woman nerved herself for the occasion. Levelling her glasses at the offender, she executed the nearest imitation of a smile she could command, and retorted,

"I am afraid, Miss Moseley, your Paris education has hardly made you understand your position in this country," then without waiting for a possibility of a reply, Mrs. De Driby swept away in her magnificence, trumpeting in her wrath like an irate elephant.

The blood rushed to Katie's temples, and her little hands for a few seconds made wild work with her pocket-handkerchief. She knew she had been worsted in an encounter with her bitterest foe. What gall that is to women, women only understand; it is vinegar to them to be beaten in such encounters at all times, but verjuice pure and unadulterated when the victor is of their own sex. Katie could have cried with vexation; but they never do that. Commend me to a woman for bearing social punishment unmoved. We male creatures whimper much more over our hurts. She has had her day's pleasure, and in the silence of her bed-chamber may ask whether *le jeu vaut la chandelle.*

CHAPTER X.

"THE WOLF DINES WITH THE LAMB."

THE heart of Piccadilly throbs strong; the fitful pulse of Bond Street knows no rest. Carriage after carraige rolls home with its freight from the Park. The tide of pedestrians ebbs, flows, and eddies between Apsley House and the Regent Circus, anon whirling fiercely up Park Lane, then sweeping with more tranquil movement down decorous St. James's towards Marlborough House and the Palace. It is about eight o'clock on a fine July evening.

With a light dust coat thrown over his evening dress, Jim Halden saunters in his usual listless way up St. James's Street, crosses into Bond Street, and makes his way leisurely towards Long's Hotel. He is on his way to dine there with Fortie Merrington. That gentleman had duly benefitted by the invitation he had accepted on the occasion of the Greenwich dinner, and this had rapidly led to considerable intimacy between them. Halden could be an amusing companion enough when he chose to exert himself. He had seen much of this world's wickedness, and could expatiate pleasantly enough on his experiences thereof, when it suited him to do so. Fortie, like most young men, had a weakness for the *chroniques scandaleuses* of London life, all of which I need scarcely say the Honourable Jim had at his finger ends, to say nothing of having been a personal actor in two or three of by no means the most venial of such histories. It was true Fripley Furnival was an equally instructive associate on these points; but then Furnival, though in an irregular way, did follow the pursuit of literature, and his time was often engaged. Halden, on the contrary, seemed to have come into this world for no apparent object; to be intensely bored with it, and to be only too glad to assist or be assisted in killing the time that hung so lamentably heavy on his own hands. So there had sprung up a close intimacy between those two, based simply on the fact that they were both idle men, and had so drifted together, much as ships do in a calm. No force directing, the same principle applies both to animate and inanimate bodies. The loungers of any watering place will exemplify what I mean.

Jim Halden sauntered slowly up the steps of Long's, in utter oblivion that his presence had attracted the attention of a sleek individual in a tall shiny hat, who had been previously engaged in sucking the top of a short stick in an indolent manner on the pavement outside. But before he was well into the entrance hall, the individual in question turned sharply, followed him, and tapping him on the shoulder, remarked,

"All right, Mr. Halden, you're my prisoner."

The Honourable Jim's countenance changed not a muscle as he turned leisurely and confronted his assailant. He looked him over quietly, and then calmly observed,

"Never saw you before. What's your d——d name, in the first place?"

"Which it's Noakes, of Cursitor Street, Sheriff's Officer, County of Middlesex," replied the other, equally unmoved.

"Happy to make your acquaintance, Noakes, though perhaps under rather unfavourable circumstances. I like a man who answers to the point. Now then, whose suit, and how much?"

"Solomon and Levy; one eighty and costs."

"Step in here for a moment. Waiter, get me some sherry-and-bitters. What do you feel like, Noakes?"

"Well, sir, I think I'll have a rinse of brandy-and-water."

"What do the costs come to?" inquired Halden, as the waiter departed to perform his order.

"Seventeen, thirteen and six," replied the sheriff's delegate.

"Waiter," inquired Halden, as that functionary returned with the required liquids. "Mr. Merrington has not arrived yet, has he?"

"No, sir; called in on his way home to dress just now. Said you was to be told he should be ten minutes late or so."

Halden leisurely sipped his sherry-and-bitters, apparently wrapped in thought. At last he said,

"Hum, I think I have it. Noakes, do you want to make a tenner easy?"

"Well, sir," grinned that worthy, "I'm sure I'm agreeable, if I sees my way clear. I don't want to inconvenience a gentleman any more than I'm obliged."

"Then finish that brandy-and-water sharp, and ring the bell. Show me up to the room Mr. Merrington has engaged," said Halden, as the waiter appeared in answer to the summons.

"Yes, sir, this way, please, sir," and he conducted them to an upstairs sitting-room, with a couple of windows looking over Bond Street, in which a dinner had been laid for two.

"Thanks. Now look here, Noakes, there's no exit from this room except by the windows or the door. The windows are a great deal too high to jump out of without breaking one's neck, consequently I can only come out by the door. I'm going to dine here with a friend, you can have a chair in the passage to watch the door so that I can't leave without your knowledge. I'll make that all right with the waiters. You're stopping to see me on business. Now here's ten pounds down if you'll delay this arrest for three hours, and then make it in here for four hundred pounds instead of one eighty and costs."

"Don't see your little game, Mr. Halden," returned Noakes, after turning the matter over in his mind for some seconds.

"Don't suppose you do; but you've made your capture, I haven't the least intention of escaping. On the contrary, shall most likely make a good thing of it. You've a tenner down, here it is," and Halden fluttered a bank note before the officer's eyes, "for sitting three hours in that passage."

"Ten pound's a deal of money," muttered Noakes, "I don't know. You'll give your word it aint a plant?" he continued, dubiously.

"Not on you, I'll swear; but look sharp, my friend will be here directly, and then it will be too late."

"Give us hold," said Noakes, holding out an avaricious claw for the tempting note. "I'll chance it. I'll act on the square with you and not come in till it's struck eleven. Mind you do the right thing too, sir!"

"All on the straight, I give you my honour. Now clear out, and keep out of the gentleman's way as he comes upstairs. Waiter," continued the Honourable Jim, "let this man stay outside, I shall want him later in the evening."

The waiters at Long's are little wont to be surprised at the eccentricities of their patrons.

It was at the other great caravanserai of batchelorhood, lived that member of the fraternity, whose vocation was so touchingly described in that quaint old lyric of bye-gone days beginning,

"My name is John Thomas, the waiter at Limmers'es,
At the corner of Conduit Street, Hanover Square;
My sole occupation is filling of brimmerses,
To solace young gentlemen laden with care."

Still his brethren of Long's devote a good deal of their time to assuaging the woes of young England's life by similar remedies. It takes a good deal to produce any feeling of astonishment on the part of these hardly tried, well drilled servitors.

Jim Halden divested himself of his coat and hat, and sat down tranquilly to await the advent of his host. He had not to wait many minutes ere he heard a quick light step on the stairs, and Fortie entered.

"Awfully sorry to have kept you waiting, Jim; but I got away from the Park so late. Yes, dinner at once," he added, to the white neckclothed official's mute appeal.

"Don't apologize, only just got here myself."

"Well, come along and sit down. Told you there was no one to meet you," and Fortie began ladling out the soup.

"Rather a relief, one gets so bored by big dinners towards the end of the season; besides, it's too hot for them unless you migrate to Greenwich or Richmond.

In a *tête-à-tête* you've no row, are not obliged to scream if you want to say anything, and one does get waited upon. I know I dined the other day at Blanton's, got literally nothing to eat. Not half servants enough, and I was too tired to shout at 'em."

"You're quite right. Now this is quiet, cool and comfortable. Come along with the champagne, waiter."

"Nothing much going on," remarked Jim. "Odd if there was, people all too languid to get into scrapes; there's Mrs. Clarke Fletcher can't summon up energy to run away with young Rawlinson, she meant it at one time, I should think—he, poor young beggar, gone past redemption, hopeless case of spoon, and's fool enough to only wish she would."

"No, the season is pretty well played out; it's getting about time to cut it. Where to is the question—you know Baden, Homburg and all these places?"

"Rather. Unlike Tom Protherton's

dog; I could tell stories about most of 'em."

"What's the joke about Tom Protherton's dog?" inquired Fortie.

"Never heard that story? It's rather good; they dev'lish near laughed old Protherton out of the Carlton with it. Pity they didn't, he's about the biggest bore in it—fellow who is always buttonholing the unwary, to inflict on them interminable stories which never have a point. In an evil moment, he accepted from somebody one of those Pomeranian dogs with the tightest tail that ever was curled. I believe Furnival was the originator of the joke; but Alec Leicester was the man who practically adapted it to the suppression of a nuisance, and on the old villain perpetrating his next outrage, exclaimed, 'My dear Prothero, I never can hear a tale of yours without thinking of your dog.'

"'My dog! why what do you mean?'

"'Mean! pooh! nonsense! man, you

can't be ignorant of what all London has decreed, that you're never to tell a story again without your dog being there, so that one may have a chance of seeing the two stiffest tales in London unfolded together.'

"The chaff spread everywhere, and 'where's the dog,' saluted old Prothero whenever he attempted one of his endless narratives."

"Jove! not bad;" said Fortie, "help yourself, and send the claret across. What cursed luck I had the other night."

"Ah, at whist—yes; paper run against you. Didn't have a very good time myself, though cards rather helped me through at the finish."

"Come in;" said Fortie, as a pair of knuckles drummed heavily on the door.

Halden glanced at the clock which was on the stroke of eleven, and taking out his cigar-case observed, "Time for a weed."

"Hallo! what the devil do you want?" inquired Fortie, as the door opened and Mr. Noakes cautiously insinuated his body into the room.

"Beg pardon, sir; I hates to disturb gentlemen at dinner, so I've waited a bit till I heard coffee was all over right and comfortable; but I've a little bit of business there with Mr. Halden that won't keep any longer."

Halden, who had by this time lit his cigar, turned leisurely round in his chair, and said, "Well, my man?"

Noakes advanced, and handing him a strip of parchment replied,

"Caption—Solomon and Levy—Four hundred and costs."

"D—d scoundrels!" exclaimed Halden, "they swore this should wait till the end of the month. I told them I couldn't meet it before, but that it would be all right then."

"Can't help it, Mr. Halden—I knows nothing about that. My orders is to bring you or the blunt back, that's all I knows."

"What on earth is the matter?" said Fortie, "is it an arrest?"

"Afraid so; these sharks promised to wait till the end of the month, at which time I've made all arrangements for meeting this bill. Put not your trust in money-lenders."

The converse of the remark might perhaps have been more applicable to Jim Halden. Many of them had wept over monies parted with in that direction, and anathematized the day that made them the proprietors of the Honourable Jim's autograph.

"Jove! this won't do, you know;" said Fortie. "We can't wind up a jolly dinner like this. Look here, my man, just step outside for ten minutes and tell the waiter to get you anything you like to drink."

Mr. Noakes looked a little dubious, he glanced first at Fortie and then at his prisoner. An almost imperceptible quiver of the latter's left eye-lid decided him.

"Well," he said, "I don't want to be disobliging, but it aint business this here, howsomever I don't mind for ten minutes or so; but mind, gentlemen, I can't be kept waiting all night."

No sooner was the door closed than Fortie exclaimed,

"Hang it all, Jim! can't anything be done about this business?"

"It's hard lines," responded Halden, "very hard lines. I've worked all I knew to get this four hundred together, and they promised me to wait till the end of the month for it. Now," he continued, plaintively, "the brutes make this arrest —they know it will add another fifty or so to my debt. I did think at last I should be clear of the vultures; but now it's all over," and putting down his cigar, the Honourable Jim leant his head on his hands in a most lugubrious manner.

Halden had not studied men and their dispositions for nothing. Neither could anyone accuse him of having altogether thrown away his opportunities at the theatres. He did his quiet despair in an artistic fashion, that no actor of light comedy could have surpassed. The feelings of his auditor were thoroughly aroused, at the sight of his calm cynical friend breaking down in this fashion.

"Pooh! nonsense! old fellow," cried Fortie, "fill your glass and let's talk it over, I dare say we can square it after a little confabulation. No use being down in your luck about it."

Halden filled his glass and shook his head moodily.

"Look here;" continued Merrington. "You say you are safe to have this money by the first of next month?"

Jim nodded assent.

"Well, if you will promise to let me have it back then, I can find it for you now. It'll take all I've got and I shall have to a little overdraw my account to boot; but that won't matter for three weeks or so."

"By Jove! Merrington, you are a good fellow. I couldn't have asked you to do this, but if you can manage it you will be doing me a great turn. It will be all right again the beginning of next month."

The bell was rung, a pen and ink brought, and while Fortie wrote out a cheque for four hundred, Halden scrawled his I.O.U. for a similar amount. Mr. Noakes was summoned and the cheque laughingly handed to him. But here arose a little difficulty.

"No doubt," said Mr. Noakes, "this here piece of paper is werry much to be preferred to Bank of England notes, being quite as good and raythcr more portable. But cheques ain't money, least-ways so we are taught in our perfession. 'Spose gen'man I takes this back to my employers and find it a regular Aldgate Pump one, what do you think they'd say to that. Why it'd be ruin to me, it would"

"Confound it!" said Fortie, as he rang the bell, "they'll give us cash for it in the house. Waiter, send the landlord here."

This produced the managing clerk of the establishment, who stating that the proprietor had gone some hours before, desired to know if he could be of any use upon the occasion. But Fortie's request staggered him. He apologised, and said that he had not so much at command. It was not probable that he had, but in any case it was hardly to be supposed that he would cash a cheque of that extent, without ascertaining beforehand whether it was good for the amount. The Honourable Jim Halden was pretty well known at Long's, and his being an intimate friend of the drawer of the cheque was not calculated to inspire confidence. It was true Merrington was also an *habitué* and had always paid his way, but an order for four hundred cash was rather a different thing from one for a *carte blanche* dinner and unlimited dry champagne and claret.

The managing clerk was dismissed, Fortie really distressed, Noakes inexorable. But Jim Halden's mind rose to the occasion. It was by no means the first time he had been inconvenienced by such *contretemps*. He was still master of the situation.

"Tell you what we'll do, Fortie. You don't mind spending the night in the passage at half-a-sovereign an hour, eh Noakes?"

"No," grinned that worthy, "not if it's twenty-four hours long."

"Good, then go back on those terms. I don't feel a bit like bed, do you? Scribble a line over to Hamilton at the 'Thalamus,' he's safe to be there; ask him to come over and bring one or two other fellows, and we'll have a regular night at whist."

"Great idea," replied Fortie. "An inspiration, by Jove! Jim, you're a genius, and we'll play till the banks are open."

The note was sent, and Hamilton, with two or three equally reckless despisers of the laws of Nature, soon made their appearance. The consumption of grilled bones, soda-and-brandy, cigars, &c., with the concomitants of unlimited chaff and continuous whist carried that scapegrace crew on in their wild revel till long after the breakfast hour of the decent London citizen; and when with throbbing temples, Fortie threw open the shutter and let in the glare

"Of babbling, gaudy and remorseless day,"

his cheque was cashed, he had been indoctrinated into high play, and naught was left him but a splitting headache to remind him of that pleasant evening with Jim Halden.

CHAPTER XI.

THE ACTRESS AT HOME.

A MODEST little house in the vicinity of the Regent's Park, constituted the home of Lizzie Jerningham. To speak more truthfully her dwelling place bordered on Baker Street, or, as the denizens of that district delight to render their address, she was of Blank Street, Portman Square. People of those parts are wont to cling to the latter as forming part of their direction. It is supposed to throw the halo of its own heavy respectability over a wide radius. Though for the matter of that, a certain Mr. Thomas Moore, not altogether unrecognised among the songsters of Britain, lived for some two or three years in George Street, a thoroughfare that in appearance is far from poetic. I never pass the house without a smile, at thinking that the Catullus of his day lived, when writing those amorous effusions, in that grimy-looking second floor. The vignettes of Slopperton accord more with one's idea of the dwelling place of the author of Lalla Rookh, &c.

The comforts of that home, such as they were, and the unpretentious little household was well to do, were in great part owing to Lizzie's histrionic labours. Her father, a music-master by profession, had run away with the daughter of a clergyman at the time under his tuition. Such a social outrage was not to be tolerated, and poor Mrs. Jerningham's relations at once washed their hands of, and wept over, her. Music-masters find a living hard to come by in London, and the bitter struggles incumbent on genteel poverty, in the course of a few years, broke down Mrs. Jerningham's naturally delicate constitution. A family came, as a family invariably does when there is little to keep them on, and the poor lady, to add to her woes, had to mourn the loss of two little ones which a kind Providence had taken early from the vale of tears and short commons they had entered upon. There remained to her now but two children, Lizzie, just in the commencement of her twenty-second year, and who was now fairly installed as one of the minor idols of the hydra-headed and capricious British Public, and the youngest of all, a boy at school.

The buffeting of the world, the low estimate that that world had formed of his capabilities, and the perpetual struggle to keep the wolf from the door, had long reduced poor Mr. Jerningham to a humble and spiritless frame of mind. Such work as he now obtained, he performed much as the mill-horse goes through his allotted labour. No uncommon type. The lofty aspirations of youth are seldom realized, and it is but too often we see that the daily labour that forms the heritage of man has lapsed into mere drudgery. He presents that mournful converse of what should be the reality of life, the working to live, instead of living to work. Men who have thus failed, look according to their good or evil natures with either intense admiration or splenetic envy upon those whose exertions in the great arena have been crowned with success. Poor Mr. Jerningham had had his sunny dream-land like most of us, and pictured himself at a West End theatre conducting the orchestra in the most perfectly fitting kids.

The success of his daughter, as an actress, threw a stream of sunshine on his prosaic life. To do him justice, he really little regarded the increased comforts of home which her now tolerably liberal salary allowed. He was wrapped up in her success. He had failed, it is true himself, but he lived again in the triumphs of his daughter. To see her act, to see the audience enchained by her art, and listen to the plaudits that rewarded one of her happiest efforts, was elysium to the heretofore broken-spirited man. It was on this point only Lizzie thwarted him. He would have been well content to play second violin in the orchestra, and witness his darling's success, believing firmly as he did that she was the first comedy actress in London. But Lizzie was inexorable. She could not bear the idea of her father figuring in such an inferior position to herself at her theatre.

"Anywhere else, father dear, and I don't mind," she was wont to say; "but I won't be a swell in a place in which you are nobody. Come and see me whenever you like. I love to think you are looking on at my successes, but not from the orchestra. Of course I can always get orders for you. If you insist on keeping up an engagement at some theatre, let it be any one but mine."

Mr. Jerningham was an honest hard-working man, and scorned to be entirely beholden to his daughter's exertions. He recognized, for he was troubled with a sensitive mind, the feelings with which Lizzie spoke. Sorely as it grieved him not to behold his pet nightly, he bowed to her decision, and henceforth his violin discoursed melody at a neighbouring temple of Thespis.

Lizzie, book in hand, is tramping up and down what is looked upon by the conventionalities of the house as her study.

Lizzie, to use her own expression, is "hammering at a part." She looks very handsome as she paces the room, her dark eyes sparkling, the coral lips slightly quivering as she enters upon some of the more animated bits assigned to her *rôle*. The blue-black masses of hair braided up behind in the grand old classical knot, which the ladies of this age have ignored for the hideous chignon (a fashion introduced by some leader of *ton* whose locks would scarce brook counting). The well-fitting muslin draperies which show yet shroud the lithe pliant figure. The quick rapid play of countenance, as the brows now corrugate for a moment at something she don't quite like or don't quite see how to make the most of. Anon breaking into a flood of sunshine, such as streams athwart the footlights to her admirers at the Hyacinth.

A sharp jerk of the bell interrupts Lizzie's studies. In her Bohemian life, the conventionalities are not observed with the strictness they are in the more melancholy superstrata of excessive respectability. She quietly opens the door to hear who the caller may be, and as the inquiry of, Miss Jerningham at home, reaches her ears, steps into the passage and says,

"Yes, Mr. Merrington; and very glad to see you. Step in here and sit down, though I can't ask you to stay long, for I've got all that to learn," and Lizzie pointed to the book she had just thrown down.

"Yes, I know your time is of value to you. You shall tell me to go whenever you want to get to work again. But I haven't seen you for nearly a week, so thought it time to come and pay my devoirs. You haven't been in the park for a mouthful of fresh air the last few days."

"No, the truth is I have a good deal to get up, and poor mother has been so unwell lately that the little time I have had to spare I have devoted to her. How's Mr. Furnival? 'The Ball on the Roll' still runs so well that I don't know when there will be a chance for his piece."

"Oh, Fripley's very well, he says it's all your fault, for if your Rose Delmar wasn't so good, people would have tired of 'The Ball' some weeks back. Says he'll never forgive you if you don't do as much for him."

"Ah, Mr. Merrington;" laughed the

actress, "tell him to mind the part is as good, and I'll promise he shan't have to complain of me. But what have you been doing lately?"

"Well! besides bewailing your absence in the park, I've been knocking about with Jim Halden a good deal—you know him?"

"Yes, very slightly; but that's even more than I care for. Don't be offended, Mr. Merrington, when I say that the less you see of Mr. Halden the better."

"Why?" inquired Fortie, with some astonishment.

"Never mind the why," retorted Lizzie. "Women are never expected to give their reasons. Still I do know a story or two about Mr. Halden, that are to say the least of it very little to his advantage."

She might have spoken in stronger terms, for Lizzie, among her acquaintances, numbered one on whom the Honourable Jim had brought unutterable woe.

"Jim is a loose fish I know," mused Fortie, "but I don't think there is any harm in him beyond he is such an unlucky fellow."

"Accept that then as an omen. Mistrust him, because his star is not in the ascendant," replied the actress, laughing; "but time's up. I don't want to be inhospitable, but I must get those words into my head."

"I bow to the necessity while I deplore it," returned Fortie, rising, "I hope you will indulge yourself with a run on Sunday."

"Yes, mind you are there to be my cavalier. Bring Fripley with you if you can. I want to talk to him about this new piece of his. Good bye," and Lizzie and her visitor shook hands.

It may easily be inferred from the foregoing, that Fortie and Lizzie Jerningham had seen a good deal of each other since that memorable dinner at Greenwich. The actress was fond of an hour in the Park after her early dinner, before the theatre once more claimed her for its own, and Merrington had been a constant and favoured attendant on such occasions. His habitual courtesy won on a girl, who was often repelled by the freedom men thought her position justified in their relations towards her. Don't think there was any *tendresse* either on her part or his in this seeming intimacy; she was quite as well pleased to meet and walk with her old ally, Fripley Furnival. People utterly unacquainted with stage life, are wont to come to the conclusion that an actress from her profession must, of necessity, be of light character. Their want of charity is proportionate with their ignorance on the subject.

Ah, ye mothers of the middle classes, in whom this idea so strongly predominates, instead of turning up the whites of your eyes, and in the old Pharisaical spirit thanking God that ye are not as this woman, ponder over the the statistics of the Divorce Court, and consider whether you ever worked as hard or were ever called upon to withstand anything like the temptation of your sisters of the stage. Before clothed in your garments of virtue and purity you condemn; see to it that your own ranks in proportion produce no more erring sheep, than that luckless profession which you at once admire and affect to despise. But when did woman ever set in judgment on woman and show mercy.

Fortie mused a good deal over what the actress had said on the subject of Halden. "Devil of a sell," he soliloquized, "if Jim's not all right—makes that four hundred look fishy, and I shall want it badly by the first of next month. Whist and écarté too ain't as kind as they were at starting, t'other way on altogether just now."

Here Fortie's musings were interrupted by a collision with a passing passenger who exclaimed.

"Reckon, stranger, counting the eyelet-holes in your boots ain't judgmatical when you're walking about this metropolis. Beg pardon, Mr. Merrington, didn't see it was you, I always go in for being first in abuse in case of collision, though I guess my own top lights were turned in the wrong direction this spell," and Seth Thorndale, for such was the speaker, shook hands heartily with Fortie.

"Glad to see you again, thought you must have returned to America," replied the latter, "as I have never come across you since Basinghall's dinner."

"Off next week; I have had a regular good look at all your theatres, and I tell you, you ain't a patch upon us for accommodation, arrangement, and comfort. You've more good actors and actresses than we have, but you've adopted the sensational drama from us and that will soon thin their ranks. A real startler, such as fetches our citizens, don't require above three or four real artists—all the rest is blue fire, unlimited supers and scenery. Don't know why I'm bothering you about all this, but you see a man is no good unless his heart is in his trade, and then he can't help talking about it. My trade is spectacular representations, or any other d——d representation that is likely to catch the taste of the New York public."

"Why you'd go in for regular Barnum business then!"

"Why not? of course I should, if it produced dollars. The collecting of dollars is the great principle of trade. This side, you have a lot of people who are always talking about the improvement of the masses. Well, let 'em improve them. A manager only caters for the public, and in his own interest tries to provide the public with the entertainment they want. When they go in for the intellectual, they'll find it all ready for them at the Cracknell Theatre, New

York; but as long as they like sensation, sensation it is to the biggest extremity I can give 'em with safety to their minds and the theatre."

"Well," laughed Fortie, "I suppose you're right. What attracts must be your first consideration."

"Gospel truth as ever you spoke; don't matter what you deal in, all you've got to do is to find out what fetches the top of the market in your line, whether it's sensational dramas, sensational novels, pedigree wheat, high-bred cattle, or gaudy calicos."

"Ah, I should like to see that country of yours."

"Do, sir, do. It'll open your eyes, it will. I don't mean to say there ain't some of your institutions here but what I think better than ours; but if you want to see a country where, if a man has gumption and grit in him to start with, he need never remain poor, just run over and stay for a spell under the star-spangled banner. Our eagle may be a young bird, but he's pretty strong in the pinions, and flies high, he does."

"Well, I must say good-bye and pleasant voyage to you."

"Thank you, sir. Recollect whenever you come to see our Great Republic—and, mind, you ain't half done travelling or seen the world till you have—you look up Seth Thorndale. Any one in New York, nearly, will tell you where to find me. I'll give you as good a dinner as ever you sat down to; right glad to see you, and you shall know what terrarpin soup, soft shell crabs, and canvas-back ducks mean. Don't forget; and now good-bye, Mr. Merrington."

And with a hearty shake of the hand they separated. Little did Fortie think then under what circumstances he should next meet Seth Thorndale.

CHAPTER XII.

LONDON IN AUGUST.

HORACE DE DRIBY at St. Helens is moodily cogitating over a letter which had arrived by that morning's post. It was from Mr. Richard Phinny, and contained the curt announcement that some of Fortie Merrington's paper had at last appeared in the market, and requested instructions regarding it. That astute solicitor further observed that one bill was the invariable precursor of many, and they might now be looked for much as dead leaves in autumn. Horace twists the letter about in his restless fingers. What he has looked and hoped for seems in a fair way to come to pass.

Still meditating, the Rector looks down

a long vista, and sees himself enthroned lord of St. Helens. He thinks over many improvements he will effect in the estate, when his reign shall have commenced. What a different course he will pursue from Sir Giles. How, instead of standing aloof in cynical disdain, he will take his place in the county, and become a political power therein. Horace is conscious of talent and latent power to become a leader amongst men. Angrily he reflects that the profession his uncle has compelled him to embrace shuts him out from the political arena, and thinks but for that the day might have come when he should have represented the county in Parliament.

Strong, stern, and ambitious, he feels little personal animosity towards Fortie. He regards him merely as an obstacle that must be swept from his path. Feeling of kith he had none. With all the relentless purpose of his race he had determined to crush him, not from any individual dislike, but as one who looked inimical to his interests and aggrandizement. His resolution on the point was as immovable and uncompromising as the old Roman dictum, *delenda est Carthago.* Merrington must be ruined. But how? he had mapped that out roughly as yet. As aforesaid, he had calculated upon Fortie's sensuous, pleasure-loving disposition, and want of firmness of character. The result was, even now showing the accuracy of his prescience. What ought to be his first move. To wait and watch had been his original determination. So far it had been successful. Was the time come for more active measures? He thought not.

"I may as well tell Phinny, at all events," he muttered, "to get possession of all the bills the young imbecile may throw into the market. It is well to hold the strings that move the puppet, even if it is not advisable to pull them.

The rope is hardly long enough yet, but the coils circle fast, as Phinny says, when the beginning is once made. I don't want him to tell me that, though if any one should be a judge of such matters it is he. H—m, it's hard to predict, but I daresay Sir Giles will bear this next attack on his purse-strings. When a man has but one weakness, he hugs it closely, and besides partiality for Fortie, no mortal could accuse my cynic uncle of another. My mother talks about the fancy he has taken to that chit of a Moseley girl. As Johnson said of the Twickenham wasp, when Boswell asked him what Pope meant by a certain line, 'He hoped, sir, it would annoy somebody.' Sir Giles patronizes Kate Moseley much on that principle, with an eye, perhaps, to my mother in particular. No! many a winning game is thrown away from want of patience. I'll just write half-a-dozen lines to Phinny, and then wait."

And how, these last two or three weeks,

has it fared with Fortie? He has so far expanded his mind, that he has imbibed all the first rudiments of play under the tuition of Halden. It has proved more exciting than lucrative, and Fortie has paid pretty smartly for his initiation. The 1st of August has come and gone, and brought forth no question of the repayment of the four hundred lent at Long's. On the contrary, Merrington now is nearly as much indebted to his Mentor as that, though Halden can't, of course, in decency press for payment. The Honourable Jim is not much given to the toleration of outstanding accounts, when the ledger shows a balance in his favour. But he handles the pigeons that fall into his hands with consummate skill, and generally reserves the quill feathers for the final plucking. His victims find the world grow cold before they discover they are unable to fly.

It is a time of much mental perturbation to the *jeunesse dorée* of London life, when comes that first awful discovery of their inability to lay their spendthrift hands upon a five-pound note. The sky lifts as their more initiated associates first introduce them to the Eleusinian mysteries of "bills." Once more the reckless revellers pursue their Circean orgies, careless of the quick gathering storm-clouds. But the tempest soon breaks, and the usurious wolf has his fangs fast in the throat of the impecunious lamb—black lambs perchance, but none the less despairing and hopeless in the merciless clutches they are now writhing in. *Reculer pour mieux sauter* is an axiom in money lending. The accommodating discounter, when he deems his time come, has generally resolved on a relentless worry, and leaves not his victim till the bones are picked clean.

It has been said that man never knows how quickly two months can pass, till he has drawn a bill at sixty days' sight with some slight misgivings at starting about meeting it when it falls due. No such thoughts clouded Fortie's mind in his pleasant career on his road to ruin. Money goes and comes back is a fact patent to all who play. The run was against him just now, but of course luck must turn. As Halden said, whist and écarté always come round if you stick steadily to the same stakes. As far as he, Halden, was concerned they did, and pretty generally to his advantage. He had never been accused of foul play, though undoubtedly of sharp practice, and he unmistakably was a scientific performer at most games that conduced to the acquisition of that lucre, for which those bottomless pockets of the Honourable Jim were ever agape.

So believing his Mentor that the wheel must turn, acknowledging the fact that,

> "Cards will run the contrary way,
> As well is known to all who play,
> And dice will conspire in season,"

Fortie steadily persevered in his sacrifices to the capricious goddess, Fortuna.

Yes, he had found something to do at last, as many others of his kind had found before him. One might paraphrase the old saying, Get money honestly if you can, but never hope to get it by gaming. The few who have done so are continually cited, but we don't hear of the thousands that have succumbed to the cards, the dice, and the race-course. How very few men can play whist, or are really good judges of racing. What thousands believe in their whist, and their talent for "spotting the winner." Earthenware jugs amongst the brass pots, can you not take the old fable to your hearts?

Town is getting very hot and very dusty. People are flying to the salt water—to the Moors—to bracing Switzerland—to wicked, but pleasant Baden—athletic young men are greasing their boots, and vainly endeavouring to condense the necessaries of dress and toilet into practicable knapsacks. The park is well-nigh deserted, and acquaintances, when they meet you, think it necessary to explain their intentions of immediate emigration. Fortie Merrington still lingers—why? Sir Giles has written rather peremptorily to request his presence at St. Helens. Preparations are making for the feast of St. Partridge, and there is to be a gathering at the Manor House. Still the fatal fascination chains him. The cards and the dice-box have thrown their glamour around him, and though it is but a few weeks since he thoroughly tasted the excitement of high play—it was with those who took care he should be artistically blooded. The wild spirit of his father runs riot in his veins, and in six short weeks Fortie has learnt to feel the day flat and spiritless till he reaches the fatal green table.

It was towards the end of October that I once met a genial Hussar acquaintance of mine. He had acquired, I forget just now how, the rather unexpected possession of four hundred pounds, and confided to me that he was only waiting for the ratification of his leave to pick up three good horses, and then have a "good time," he hoped, in the Atherstone country. Dire procrastination. An evening in town is so dull in October. One must do something. He selected whist for his pastime, and when on the fourth morning he received his leave *en règle*, had succeeded in getting through three hundred and eighty at the fascinating game. I don't think he hunted with the Atherstone, and rather fancy that an odd day with harriers on a pony was his lot that winter.

Sauntering moodily up St. James's Street one afternoon, Fortie ran against Fripley Furnival. He had hardly seen him for some weeks past.

"Halloa, young 'un," said that gentleman, "you look faded and seedy. What the devil keeps you in town? I thought you had left, like all other elements of civilization. Haven't seen you for ages, what on earth have you been doing?"

"Glad to see you, Fripley; but as to why I'm in town I might ask you the same question."

"Me? Oh, I've taken Tom Donaldson's post as sub-editor of the *Argosy* till the end of the month. He was getting real ill, poor beggar—change was a necessity for him. He's an old pal, so I couldn't refuse, being in rude health myself; but I shall be uncommon glad to hand it over on the first. What sort of a party had you at Goodwood?"

"Very pleasant; I enjoyed myself much."

"Come and have a turn in the Park and tell me all about it," said Fripley, slipping his arm through Merrington's. "Who had you?"

"Halden, Hamilton, Laurence Finucane, Tom Sloper, of the —th Hussars, and a Baron Bartini, of whom I don't know much."

"Never heard of the Baron, myself;

but by Jove, Master Fortie, if you weren't in with a nice lot I never heard of them. A quartette of more reckless gamblers than those you have mentioned, would be hard to name in all London. How did you come through on the week?" and Furnival looked a little inquisitively at his companion.

"Very well as regards the racing. Tom Sloper and the Baron were either right good judges, or in possession of some very good information. I followed them pretty much, and did tidily during the days, but I couldn't hold my own at night."

"Cards, I suppose?"

"Yes, we always played railway whist after dinner."

"Fortie, my son, you take my advice, and eschew railroad whist for the present; a game in which honours are nil, and points only count, is rather too great a pull for the best players. Can't say regarding the Baron, but Halden and

Hamilton were almost bound to be winners at that. Anything else?"

"Yes, we generally wound up with a little 'chicken.'"

"Another snare I should counsel you to keep clear of. I am afraid, Fortie, I didn't do you a good turn when I introduced you to Halden. Bear in mind he's not much to be trusted."

This was locking the stable-door a little late with a vengeance. The time for such counsel had gone by, and though Furnival was by no means aware of the harm that had come of it, yet it had been a very fatal hour for Fortie in which he had made the acquaintance of Halden.

"Oh, I don't know," he replied, "I rather like Jim, he don't affect to be anything but what he is. I've seen a good deal of him lately."

"Well, it's no use talking about it now, Fortie, but seeing a good deal of Jim Halden, as a rule, is not good for the generality of his associates. When did you see Lizzie Jerningham last?"

"Not very lately. What with Goodwood and other engagements, I have had my hands pretty full this last three weeks."

"I also have not been about. What with the responsibilities of the *Argosy*, and other literary work of my own, I have had a busy time this last month. Somebody told me you had got in at the Thalamus."

"Yes, thanks to your interesting yourself in my behalf. I like it much better than the Areopagus. It's so much more sociable; besides, I hardly knew a soul in the latter, and have often thought the Sarcophagus would be a more approximate name for it, as far as I was concerned."

"Good, that's not a bad joke for your age. Quite good enough for the smoking-room of that dreary and venerable institution. But whither do you fly when you leave this. I presume even your hours here are now numbered; you've drained the season to its very dregs."

"Off next week to my uncle's in Lincolnshire for the shooting. Shan't have above ten days to wait till that comes on. If you've nothing better to do, you'd better join our party at St. Helens, Fripley."

"I tell you what, I rather like that idea. I must get out of town, and can't quite settle where to go. Will you have me *en vérité?*"

"Yes, and delighted to catch you. We've lots of birds. I can guarantee the claret, and you'll suit Sir Giles down to the ground. It will be a tolerably pleasant party. Put it down, Fripley."

"It's a match," returned the other, "and I'll make my number at St. Helens as soon after the first as I can."

"All right, and now good-bye. Don't suppose I shall see you again before we meet there," and Fortie made his way through Albert Gate.

Fripley wandered on, past the Knightsbridge Barracks, where the sentries made one hot to look upon, crossed the bottom of the Ladies' Mile near Kensington Gardens, and strolled listlessly back on the other side. This steaming August evening the park seems well nigh deserted. I speak comparatively, for there are many who are unable to withdraw their necks from the collar these hot summer days, and "the lungs of the metropolis" are never empty. But the froth and vanity of the season have betaken themselves to the Moors, the country, Folkestone, Brighton, and the Continent. Ramsgate, Hastings, all the South Coast watering places, Derbyshire and the Lake country are flooded with the great city's out-pourings—out-pourings of a shade less pretension, with whom a ticket for the Queen's ball is by no means an object of paramount importance. Margate, Gravesend, &c., are surging over with another grade of the annual overflow, a class to whom sands, shrimps, buff slippers, tea-gardens and assembly-rooms are primary objects, when they temporarily vacate their cells in the great London hive. All this outflow naturally makes an impression, and on no part of the metropolis is it so vividly impressed as upon Hyde Park. A turn by the side of Rotten Row is wont to produce feelings of acerbity during the vacation. Repinings at our lot, much discontent that we are not elsewhere, and an aggrieved feeling of being somehow "put upon" are predominant in our manly bosoms. Battersea Park is quite as pretty, equally healthy, and calls up no melancholy reminiscences, I would humbly suggest to those so afflicted.

Fripley was a victim to all this revulsion of feeling, as he sauntered leisurely back by the side of the deserted Row. He lit a cigar, and began to muse meditatively over Fortie Merrington and his affairs.

"Wish to Heavens," he thought, "I

had never been the means of bringing him and Jim Halden together; but it never occurred to me at the time. It's done now and can't be helped. I couldn't, if I had tried, have given him a worse start in London life. I wonder how far that confounded Jim has put him wrong. No use talking to him up here, down at St. Helens he may be more amenable to reason. But I'm afraid three months of Halden's society is enough to have about ruined any young one, more especially one who has not yet chalked out a career for himself. Curse it, too, somebody told me the other day that Jim had been displaying his talents at the Thalamus, and there are too many already disposed to make a gambling house of the pleasantest night club in London. What a fool I was not to attend to Blatherwick's suggestion, and make a point of having the Honourable Jim pilled there last year."

Still meditating in this wise he crossed

the Row once more, and made his way out 'neath the Duke's statue, and ran against the very man he had been mentally castigating, in Piccadilly.

"How do, Fripley," said Halden, with his usual languid manner.

"Why, what on earth keeps you in town, Jim? I should have thought you had been away to the Moors or 'Salt Licks' three weeks back."

"No moor to go to. Nobody has seen fit to ask me, and the Governor don't mince matters, but says he'll be d—d if I set foot on his. Getting hot and slow this, though, so I'm off to Baden next week."

"The old story I suppose, experiments in the dyeing trade or fixing a colour."

"No, Fripley, I have got through my days of innocence, and don't look to making a fortune over the red or the black. But there's always money to be made at Baden. The race week is prolific in robberies, if you do but know of them. I usually get an advantageous hint or two."

"Well, good-bye, may your speculations be lucky, Jim," and Fripley wended his way east.

CHAPTER XIII.

BESS.

YES, she was a vagrant looking dog. A small, light, wiry bitch, with a coat that no care, feeding, or attention could make any other than ragged. She looked a very mendicant among dogs, with large patches of hair rubbed off her in places. She was a disreputable dog, she had a felonious manner with her, and bore petty larceny imprinted on her countenance. A joint missing, and a score of her kind about the house, she would have been convicted on her appearance. Nothing but a clear alibi could have saved her. She was a cynical dog, wont to snap viciously at those whose habiliments proclaimed them unencumbered with much of this world's gear. In her dog's wisdom; she felt they might be insulted with impunity. Vagrant herself, she endured no vagrancy in humanity. Silk and broadcloth she tolerated, welcoming them with cold politeness and unbelief.

One cannot exactly say this dog had a religion, but she had a faith, which is something as times go, and that centred in her master. This ill-conditioned looking cur was Fortie Merrington's pet retriever. He was her deity. To him she owed all pleasure, or as occasion demanded, for dog nature is no more infallible than man's, all pain. She bounded with delight at his caresses, and she was not habitually a demonstrative dog. With drooped ears, slinking tail, and meekly crouching, she came to meet the relentless punishment of her misdoings, when she could summon courage to encounter that Nemesis, which she knew so invariably followed the pursuit of the forbidden hare, or her occasional infirmities of temper. Quick and lynx-eyed as a greyhound, no schoolboy on the first day of his holidays ever ran such madcap races as she, when such little misdemeanour had been satisfactorily settled for. With pricked ears and impatient shivering, Bess sits on her haunches in the warm sunshine this August morning, anon giving an occasional whimper. She wanted no information, she knew that her master had arrived, and visions of partridge shooting and endless scampers by wood and river filled her dog mind.

Yes, Fortie Merrington has at last torn himself from the Circean goddess of the gaming table, and arrived over night at St. Helens.

Sir Giles remarked he looked worn. "Been burning the candle at both ends I suppose, as men are apt to do in their first season. We don't improve as we grow older, but we learn to economise physical powers in the pursuit of pleasure. You'll be all the better for a spell of country life again."

"Do me good, no doubt; I've been living a little quicker lately than one could be expected to last at. Is my aunt here?

"Yes, she is good enough to play lady of the house for me this month."

Fortie felt that first quiet evening at the Manor House inexpressibly tedious. The expected party had not yet assembled, and the dinner-table was limited to the trio. His aunt opined that he had left his heart in London. Her nephew being hipped and *distrait*, she jumped to the conclusion that he was in love. Women are apt to assign our liver complaints and moody reflections over unpaid bills, or unpromising Derby books, to the all-swaying power of Eros. He stands so entirely to them as the first power of the universe that they make but little account of Plutus and Nemesis, two lesser deities that a good deal more influence our masculine understandings. We spend much of our time in pursuit of the former and evasion of the latter, and for the most part with very chequered success.

However, the evening wore away. Very bored was Fortie, as he lit his cigar in the solitude of the smoking-room. One of the awful curses of the gambler's life, is that it crushes out not only all other interests, but even the natural affections—he thinks of nothing else. Society, pleasure of all kind, the home ties, the ordinary loves and likings of man, are all submerged 'neath the fierce intoxicating torrent upon which he has embarked. Merrington had conceived a strong passion for Kate Moseley. It had been sufficient to steel him even against the attractions of Lizzie Jerningham, though that they were by no means easy to resist, many men could testify. It is probable that but for that preoccupation of heart, he would not have remained insensible to the charms of the handsome actress. Much as he had thought of Kate before, since he had been launched on the whirlpool of play she had hardly crossed his mind. Absorbed in the fierce struggle for gain, he was dead to all other passions.

But now over this cigar, Kate Moseley crossed his moody mind like sunshine. What a brute he had been, all the fault of those accursed cards, &c. Yes, he would go and see Kate to-morrow—that he had not written for some time he felt guiltily conscious of.

I suppose it was not a very proper thing those two corresponding at all. I can quite fancy exception being taken to it by the rigid moralists with whom it is my privilege to associate; but then with the present postal facilities, it is so very difficult to know with whom anyone may be corresponding, that I can quite imagine a good many most uncompromising matrons do not at all realize the indiscretional correspondence into which their daughters may be betrayed. In the case of Kate and Fortie, there was no one to trouble their head about the matter.

Fortie lounges leisurely out of the hall, and pauses a moment to stare over the park with its soft thick grass. The weird, gnarled old trees are in all the full beauty and grandeur of their summer panoply. It is one of those bright still August mornings, that seem as if they had begun close on noon to start with. How one revels in mere existence midst the trees, grass, and flowers, after the hot feverish London life with its heart-burnings and jealousies. There is a sensation of peace, quiet and repose about it. Let me be in the shade and read novels, or watch the lazy hum of the insects, or listen to the distant murmurs from harvest-field or river; but breathe not a word to me of work to be done, or of energy to be summoned up.

The *dolce far niente* is the only fit sacrifice to pay to our common mother-nature to-day.

Fortie, though to a certain extent sharing this sentiment, had marked out still more golden hours for himself. He thought how pleasant it would be to lounge away the time at Kate Moseley's feet while she busied herself with some apology for work, or perhaps to read out one of those favourite authors, and listen to her lively remarks on Maude, Christabel, or Lady Geraldine's courtship.

"Bess, my woman;" he said, as he strolled to where the retriever, crouching on the ground with ears laid back and lips twitching with impatience, was switching her ragged tail, "are you glad to see me?"

As I have said before, Bess was peculiar in her ways, she neither jumped nor barked at sight of her master, but conducted herself after another fashion—turning her head from side to side;

bridling in short like a finished coquette, and ever changing the arrangement of her fore paws. The dog gave a low whimper, sprang up on him as he loosed her chain, and then careered round and round the yard like a mad thing, yelping in the exuberance of her delight. A sharp word from her master recalled her to his side. She thrusts her nose hurriedly into his hand, still quivering with anxiety for the wild gallop she has promised herself this summer morning. A wave of Fortie's hand and she is away three hundred yards in front of him—a hare dashes across her path. She pauses, looks ruefully after it for a moment, and then races back to her master, showing a fortitude in her dog nature that that master might do well to emulate.

Along the river-bank went Fortie, thinking much of Katie's blue eyes and golden hair. It was but a short time back he had strolled along that path with her. His better nature was beginning to reassert itself, and already he cursed the mad folly of the last few weeks. Then he began to ponder on what his liabilities might be for those nights of feverish pleasure. Had it been pleasure? nothing seemed like it at the time; but the excitement was over—all seemed vanity and vexation now. He soon reaches the low red-brick house by the water. Though he had not arrived unexpectedly at the Manor House, yet he had never indicated the particular day on which his advent might be looked for, so Kate could scarce know that he was once more at St. Helens. He just glances in at the low porch—the house seems deserted. Of course, Kate such a glorious morning would have betaken herself to her favourite seat at the bottom of the garden by the water's side. Quickly he threads the well-known path, the soft grass muffles his footsteps—he is right. On the rustic bench, leaning her cheek on her hand, sits Kate Moseley looking dreamily over the river. Book and work have fallen neglected on the green sward at her feet, and the girl's mind is far away lapped in the rosy visions of fancyland.

It is not till he murmurs, "dearest Kate" at her side, that she is aware of his presence. Starting to her feet, with a bright smile, she exclaimed,

"Mr. Merrington! How do you do?"

She could not disguise that she was glad to see him; for in those three months that he had been away, Kate had found out that she did care a good deal about him; but she was nevertheless conscious of having been rather neglected of late. The first of these feelings brought the sunshine into her face, as the latter impelled her to moderate her greeting.

"And is that all you have to say to me, Katie, after my absence?" continued Fortie, as the girl paused. "How do you do, Mr. Merrington?"

"Do you deserve more? Do you remember the curt half dozen lines that have responded to my later letters? Do you know, sir, that the last two have been left unanswered?" cried the girl proudly. "You know I am beneath you in station. You should have been all the more careful to prevent my realizing that fact."

"Katie, dearest, listen to reason. I have come to you as my good angel to save me from myself. I have been mad the last few weeks, and you have been sacrificed to a worthless rival."

"And you dare come here to tell me so," blazed out the girl, the blue eyes flashing, and her mobile features working with the sore wounded pride that was struggling within her. "If I was wrong to believe your protestations of love, I thought not to encounter insult at your hands—*noblesse oblige* has been deemed a proverb with your race."

"Stop! you mistake me quite. My heart has beat for no other woman but you, Katie. But I have yielded to the fascinations of play, and forgot you as I forgot all else."

The girl's face softened as he spoke, what was play compared to a feminine rival. "Oh, Fortie!" she said, "I'm so sorry," and the tears stood in the blue eyes. "I didn't understand, and you—you made me very unhappy."

"Why, you're crying, Katie. No reason for that, because I have made a fool of myself."

"I am not crying," she replied, averting her head, and angry with herself that a glistening tear-drop fell on her dress in direct contradiction to the assertion. But she said, turning again towards him. "I don't yet admit your excuse, sir. What preoccupation could justify leaving my foolish notes unanswered?"

"None—as you rightly say, if in the world's eyes you are not of my station,

I should but pay you the more deference. Don't be unkind, Katie, and let me feel that in my madness I have lost more than I ever counted on. It is bad enough as it is, I fear; but this would so eclipse the other, that that other would seem of small account," and as he spoke, Fortie stole his arm round the slender waist and possessed himself of the little hand nearest him.

Kate disengaged herself in an instant, and stood fronting him.

"Fortie Merrington," she said, "you are speaking to me as no man has a right to do to a woman, unless he has asked her to marry him. What am I to understand, I believe you loyal. You would not insult me, surely?"

Fortie's handsome face looked troubled as he replied simply.

"I knew I loved you, and thought you loved me. You never did, or you could not do me this injustice. Adieu," and he rose in his wrath, for Fortie was very much in earnest. But ere he had gone twenty paces, he could not help looking round. The small proud figure had vanished, and on the bench crouched a visibly agitated conglomeration of muslin. Katie's slight figure stood no longer erect and indignant, but prostrate on the bench the girl was giving vent to passionate sobs.

Fortie's heart failed him, in a second he was by her side once more. "Katie, I can't bear to see you cry. If you will not believe me, what can I say to you. I hoped that one day you would give me leave to call you my wife. It is you who have dared to question me on that point."

"Oh, Fortie, Fortie, will you forgive me!" said the girl, as she nestled into his arms. "I'm so miserable. I have no mother." Here her sobs half choked her. "You know I'm not of your class of life. I love you so, forgive me if I feared you might trifle with my love. Please," (no words can describe the pleading tones in which this was uttered,) "please do think how alone I stand. Forgive me now, and I will never doubt you again."

"At lovers' perjuries they say Jove laughs," and the halls of Olympus shook with laughter.

Fortie did what I fancy few men could have refrained from doing under the circumstances, he kissed the tears from the blue eyes, called her his own darling, and speedily restored sunshine to the fair face that looked up at his so fondly.

Fortie, though he genuinely loved her, had hardly intended to proceed thus far in his flirtation with Katie when he started from the Manor House.

> "Et mihi res, non me rebus, subjungere conor,"

saith the old satirist. Fallacious idea, as if "men were not ever the sport of circumstances, more especially perhaps when circumstances seem the sport of men."

And now came those sunshiny moments that come once to most of us in the course of our lives. That sweet interchange of nothings, fond questioning and foolish answering, that form the elysium of the first acknowledgment of mutual love. And Fortie made his confession of reckless folly, while Kate listened in a state of mingled admiration and terror, as he recounted those wild nights of play, which he vowed should never happen more now he was blessed with her love.

And again, loud rang the laughter through Olympian halls. Despite the misery it often entails on them, women are apt to regard a reckless gambler with a certain amount of admiration. The *beau joueur* is looked upon with a species of reverence in many salons. Amidst more decorous society, the same feeling exists mixed with horror and pity. Women cannot withhold a certain amount of admiration for recklessness in men, let it take what form it may. Moreover, most women sympathize with gambling at heart.

"But, Fortie dear, what will you do? You will have to pay all this. What will Sir Giles say?"

"Well, pet, I don't know. I could pay it perhaps without his knowledge, though it's doubtful. I haven't made up my mind about it yet. He's been a good uncle to me, and I think I shall take him into my confidence that far. But, Katie love, proud as I am of you, you must promise to keep our engagement a secret from every one for a little, till I get all these affairs settled. You'll promise me that, and trust me implicitly, won't you?"

"Yes, I promise and I trust. Yes, trust for ever, Fortie."

And for the third time, pealed high the laughter on Mount Olympus.

Fortie's reply though labial was not verbose; but paradise is not to be more than tasted in this world. A low growl from Bess called attention to that astute retriever, who had lain coiled on the grass some few yards from their feet. Her erect head, and pricked ears, told her master that somebody was approaching; and Katie and he rapidly resumed positions more in accordance with society's views of a morning call, than they were then occupying. Yes, a dog that can be depended upon is a great auxiliary in surreptituous love-making—an admirable sentry, and defies counsel in the witness box. No attorney would have thought it worth while to subpœna Bess, though nobody could have told more about, or felt more disgusted at the way in which her master had passed that bright August morning. A Bess of humanity would have scorned to let the sun go down without apprising the whole parish on the subject.

Birkett Moseley was now seen slowly approaching. The retriever cast a glance at her master. She had seen Moseley often before, but had never quite made up her dog mind in his case. She looked upon him as an interloper now, and mutely requested instructions as to whether to take a piece out of the leg of his trousers, or to welcome him with dignified reserve. Fortie's "quiet, old woman," was sufficient. Bess once more stretched herself on the grass, and submitted in a condescending way to be petted by Katie.

"Glad to see ye, Mr. Merrington, glad to see ye," said the steward, as he shook hands with Fortie. "Some of 'em told me this morning ye were back from London. Pleased ye'll be, no doubt, to get among the green fields once more, and the shooting just beginning. Ye were main fond of the shooting always. Jackson told me the other day there were more birds to year than he minds for many a season. Reckon Sir Giles is going to have the Manor House full all next month, be he not?"

"Yes, I fancy we shall have people coming and going all September. I haven't seen Jackson myself, but hear there's every chance of good sport."

"Aye, there should be; the hares have 'most grazed the 'church close' down; the sooner ye thin 'em there the better."

"Yes," chimed in Katie, "there is more game on the estate than the tenants can bear with. The hares and rabbits have made dreadful work with the crops. You and your friends, Mr. Merrington, must do your *devoir*, and abate what is becoming an injustice to the farmer."

"You little democrat," laughed Fortie. "However, Moseley, we'll devote the whole of next month to their extermination."

"Aye, do, and do it well while ye're about it. If ye don't kill 'em off closer than was done last year, I'm doubting the tenants will want something off the rents, and Sir Giles won't like to hear of that."

"Jove! no, that's not his line. He'll say they may leave if they don't like it."

"Ah, Mr. Fortie, but you should talk to him. He thinks a deal of you, and mebbe he'd listen if you spoke. He won't to me, and I tell ye the lands let at a fair value, not counting the damage the game does."

"Well," laughed Merrington, "my uncle sticks pretty firm to his own opinions. You ought to know that, if any one does. All I can do, I think, is to see that we thin the hares and rabbits as far as possible next month. Good-bye, I must be off now. Come along, Bess. Good-bye, Katie."

A warm pressure of the hand, a passionate glance, and he was gone.

"Are ye going in, lass?" inquired Moseley, as Kate began to gather up her feminine belongings.

"Yes, father; I am rather tired," and the girl walked dreamily towards the house. Arrived there, she ascended at once to her own room, and began to muse over the events of the morning.

"Yes," she muttered, "I do love him; but will they ever let me marry him? Fortie! Fortie! I don't know which of us has been most foolish. Sir Giles will never hear of it. Oh! this caste! why should I not be deemed fit bride for him?"

Here the girl walked to the glass. She looked at herself steadfastly for a minute or so,

> "Getting so by heart the beauty which all others most adore."

Apparently she was pleased with the result; the rather knit brows softened, and a smile rippled over her face as she murmured,

"'Little democrat,' he called me. Ah! love makes a pretty muddle of our democratic sentiments. Once we admit him, we become the willing slaves of utter despotism—would barter our opinions for a kind word, and change our convictions for a kiss."

END OF THE FIRST VOLUME.

LONDON:
Printed by A. Schulze, 13, Poland Street.